Go Play Outside!

Go Play Outside!
Tips, Tricks, and Tales
from the Trails

Nancy Fresco

with Elizabeth Cable, Molly Cable, and Jay Cable

SNOWY
OWL
BOOKS

University of Alaska Press Fairbanks

Text © 2021 University of Alaska Press

Published by
University of Alaska Press
P.O. Box 756240
Fairbanks, AK 99775-6240

Cover and interior design by UA Press.

Opening spread: Bear-viewing (from a safe distance) offers excitement (but not too much excitement) while tandem-biking the Denali Park Road. FAMILY PHOTO

Cover images by Nancy Fresco and Jay Cable. From the top, left to right:
    A muddy face results from no fenders on Denali Park Road.
    A backcountry cabin in Alaska's White Mountains; cabin rented by BLM.
    Organizers of a footrace on the Denali Park Road left an inspiring sign.
    An unexpected summer hailstorm on Beaver Creek.
    Tent time with daddy during a hike on the Chena Dome Trail.
    Admiring the view from a ridgeline on the 29-mile Chena Dome Trail.

Library of Congress Cataloging-in-Publication Data

Names: Fresco, Nancy, author. | Cable, Jay, author. | Cable, Elizabeth,
    author. | Cable, Molly, author.
Title: Go play outside! : tips, tricks, and tales from the trails / By Nancy Fresco
with Elizabeth Cable, Molly Cable,
    and Jay Cable.
Description: Fairbanks : University of Alaska Press, [2021]
Identifiers: LCCN 2020030580 (print) | LCCN 2020030581 (ebook) | ISBN
    9781602234390 (paperback) | ISBN 9781602234406 (ebook)
Subjects: LCSH: Outdoor recreation. | Family recreation. | Parent and
    child.
Classification: LCC GV191.6 .F74 2021 (print) | LCC GV191.6 (ebook) | DDC
    796.5 dc23
LC record available at https://lccn.loc.gov/2020030580
LC ebook record available at https://lccn.loc.gov/2020030581

The tales in this book took place primarily on the traditional and current lands of the Tanana, Koyukon, Tlingit, and Dena'ina peoples, with passage across many other Indigenous lands.

The offices of the University of Alaska Press —and indeed the State of Alaska itself— are likewise wholly located on Alaska Native lands.

We acknowledge the Alaska Native, First Nations, and American Indian lands upon which we work, play, and reside. We cherish the land on which we live and depend, and we honor and respect the people who came before us, and who are still here.

Contents

Age Sub-Zero: Planning for Kids   3

Age 0: Precious Cargo   15

Age 1–2: Large Opinions, Small Vocabularies   33

Age 3–4: Short Legs, Short Attention Spans   51

Ages 5–6: We Can Do It!   95

Ages 7–9: We Want a Vote in This   133

Age 10 and Up: Hey, Wait for the Grownups   175

Age Sub-Zero: Planning for Kids

Can Parents Still be Adventurous?

During my thirteen years of Official Parent Experience, I've been asked some variant of this question a surprising number of times— by new parents, soon-to-be-parents, and not-sure-if-we-want-to-be-parents. Free-spirited young adults seem genuinely worried that if they take on the role of "mom" or "dad," they will be locked forever in a minivan with dark-tinted windows.

"Will we still be able to enjoy the great outdoors? The wild places? The adventures?"

I can't claim to know everyone's answer, but I do know my own. It's long and complicated, and covered in myriad ways in this book. It is also short: yes.

In some ways this is a book about extremes: temperatures of fifty-four below zero, days of almost total darkness, hordes of mosquitoes, driving gales of sleet, and mile upon mile where the cell phone shows zero bars and the radio scans nothing but static. But as a family, enjoying these journeys together, we aren't focused on survivalism, suffering, or acts of grandeur. Thus, we've chosen to write about finding normalcy, sanity, and humor within those extremes.

This book is about riding bikes around town in the rain, changing diapers on a windy mountaintop, sharing broken cookies at far-flung hot springs, and persuading two toddlers to put on their snowpants. It's about sled dogs we rescued from the pound, third-hand parkas, and the many uses of zip-ties and duct tape. It's set in the heart of Alaska, but it's specific to almost anywhere. It's a how-to book, and a how-not-to book, and everything in between.

There are plenty of things for new parents to panic about. In fact, there are plenty of things for parents to panic about when they are a decade or more removed from being new at it. But the ability to enjoy the great outdoors is not one of them.

TIP ■ Not Just for Alaskans

Most of the advice and adventures shared in this volume are based in the 49th state. A few terms—and a lot of place names—may be unfamiliar or obscure. Don't let that throw you off.

Alaska is not the only place on Earth that has cold weather, or bears, or mosquitoes, or rain. Even the most temperate or urban settings offer room for exploration and adventure with kids. Every lesson we've learned, every trail game we've played, and every snack we've provided will work just as well in Washington, Wichita, or Winnipeg. So, wherever you are—go play outside!

Over the years, some of the most frequent comments we've heard are variations of "I can't believe kids are doing that!" or "My kid would never do that!" By "that," people mean hiking up the Summit Trail to Wickersham Dome, or cross-country skiing eight hilly miles to Stiles Creek Cabin, or biking to the grocery store to pick up a few supplies, or whatever else our family happens to be doing.

I could respond that kids love nature. I could argue that being outside is good for their small bodies and growing minds. I could argue that the whole world is a delightful living classroom full of many-legged arthropods, weird fungus, and rotting things under logs. Or I could simply point out that kids whine when they're indoors, too.

There are some places that feel inappropriate to take toddlers (fancy restaurants, symphonies, any movie not involving Bob the Builder) because their whining will ruin the experience for others. But as all the most morbid fairy tales suggest, the deep dark woods offer plenty of space for shrieking and frolicking unheard.

When Molly and Lizzy were younger, they didn't get much of a choice about doing "that". It was just . . . what we were doing. Maybe that makes Jay and me sound like despots—but in our own defense, most three-year-olds don't get to dictate the family's summer vacations or weekend jaunts. The kids riding around in shopping carts at Costco also likely didn't choose that as their number one preference. And, let's face it, sometimes they are making that abundantly clear.

Parenting takes patience. A LOT of patience. Parenting takes more patience than we mortals really have. But that's true no matter where and how it's done. I'll be the first to admit that taking kids on epic adventures—or even decidedly non-epic ones—requires a lot of planning, a lot of attention to detail, a few new accoutrements, and a lot of resilience in the face of dramatic childish woes. You may find yourself wandering over a mountain in the fog, simultaneously searching for the next cairn and trying to sing the entire score of The Wizard of Oz, while the small yet appallingly heavy person on your back demands more gummy worms and tells you that Dora the Explorer never gets lost, because she uses her MAP. But at least you will be able to give yourself a break from repeating, for the forty-seventh time, "Sweetie, use your INSIDE voice."

In writing this book, I'm still not sure that I have all the answers. The answers that I do have might not match many normal people's questions. We live in a cabin in the woods in the middle of Alaska. We don't have indoor plumbing. I've competed in mountainous marathons, off-road triathlons, hundred-mile mountain-bike courses, and Subarctic winter wilderness ultra-races. Jay's favorite pastime is snow-biking the thousand-mile Iditarod Trail.

Luckily, this book is not about any of that.

Don't get me wrong, I love all the ridiculous and over-the-top aspects of my life. The romantic ideal of being a Wilderness Woman is appealing. Nonetheless, it's utterly eclipsed, in my day-to-day existence, by the reality of being a middle-aged mom who commutes a couple of miles to her job at the local university, makes a lot of peanut butter sandwiches, and has holes in most of her socks. Despite the blatant oddities of our existence, I feel pretty darned normal, and so do my two thirteen-year-old co-authors.

Your kids won't love every outdoor moment. Neither will you. But the answer is still yes. Definitely yes.

Ultimately, this is a book about the joys of playing outside. And that, I hope, is something to which we can all relate.

Happy trails, new explorers.

How We Became Accidental Role Models

"So, how old were they on your first ski trip?" my friend Beth asked, gesturing toward Molly and Lizzy. The twins, then eleven, were leading the way along the not-entirely packed trail, doing their best to glide effectively on the sand-dry ten-below-zero snow.

Locations and Trail Names
Locations and trail names are included in trip descriptions mostly for the curious. More important are the details about what kind of trip it was. The distance, the type of locomotion, the weather, and the accommodations all offer hints as to what we found possible (and enjoyable) at different ages.

Moose Creek Cabin from the Haystack Trailhead
Location: White Mountains National Recreation Area.

Distance and duration ▪ 20 miles round-trip, one overnight.

Locomotion ▪ Cross-country skis, with adults pulling plastic pulk gear sleds.

Terrain ▪ Mixed hills and flats; trail mostly well broken by snowmachines and mushers, but somewhat soft in places.

Weather ▪ About -15°F and mostly clear.

Accommodations ▪ Bureau of Land Management rental cabin, equipped with a wood stove (wood gathered by foraging and water melted from snow).

"Five months," I said quickly, laughing, "We just went to Lower Angel Creek. But Tom wrote a story about the trip, for the News-Miner."

At the time, I'd assumed that no one would be terribly interested. We went to a perfectly ordinary state-owned, backcountry cabin equipped with a wood stove and lantern and located a scant four miles from the trailhead. But Jay and I humored our friend Tom Moran's request that he chronicle our "adventure."

It turns out that babies are not only photogenic—who knew?—but also scarce in the backcountry. And suddenly, after the story in the newspaper, I was—well, not famous, but Fairbanks famous. When the segment appeared, full-color in the Sunday edition, some strangers began to recognize me—in the grocery store, in the parking lot of the hardware store, at Mother Moose story time at the library. A few of them seemed horrified that I'd put my babies at risk, but most seemed inordinately thrilled. And they had questions.

People wanted to know what equipment we used, and how it worked out. They wanted to know how we could be sure the kids were warm, how we dealt with nursing them, how we managed the diaper

The twins at five months old at Lower Angel Creek Cabin, on their first back-country ski trip.
Tom Moran

situation, and whether the babies seemed to enjoy the experience. They wanted to know how they could take their kids camping, too.

I felt like a fraud. I was only five months into the parenting gig, and I was most definitely winging it. But it seemed rude to demur, so with hesitation and caveats I answered the questions anyhow.

The twins grew from babies to toddlers. Eventually, everyone forgot about the News-Miner article (except for Tom, who is quite good at organizing his archives, generous with his writing, and still willing to go on trips with us). But the questions never quite dried up.

People saw me biking the kids to preschool in a kiddie trailer at thirty below zero. They saw our mud-spattered family out on the Denali Park Road with our five-year-olds on tag-along bikes. They saw us hiking the Chilkoot Trail and the Grand Canyon with kids who looked far too small for hazardous precipices and notorious mountain passes. They saw us, a family of foreign lunatics, biking around Iceland in howling rain. And they had questions for us.

I still felt like a fraud, but I kept answering the questions. Time went by.

And then there we were, out on the trail again, eleven years later. That trip, a ten-mile jaunt from the Haystack trailhead to the BLM-managed Moose Creek Cabin, seemed just as unremarkable as the Angel Creek trip of years past. We were covering one tiny fragment of the two hundred miles of trails that loop through the White Mountains north of Fairbanks. The temperature was pretty average for a Fairbanks January day—ten or fifteen below zero Fahrenheit. Our not-so-high-tech gear included hand-me-down kids' skis, plastic sleds adapted for gear-hauling, and a couple of Thermoses of cocoa. But once again, I was being asked for advice, this time by Beth—her midriff noticeably larger than normal—and her husband Constantine.

What gear did we use when the kids were infants? What about when they were toddlers? How did we ensure safety, contentment, and parental sanity?

Jay, who loves to talk about gear almost as much as he loves to use it, launched into a plethora of detail about the things we bought, the things we made, and how it all worked out. Meanwhile, I reminisced about the complications of trying to nurse twin babies on the trail—without freezing any crucial baby-parts or any crucial me-parts, and without bonking from sheer calorie deficit.

> Mom has told me that when I was no older than the roly-poly stage, I would walk to the door at forty below and shout, "Outside!" As egregious as this sounds, I believe it, because all of my really early memories of "Outside!" are positive.
>
> "Outside" was the place I could scream as loud as I wanted, get covered with mud or snow, and give Dad not altogether helpful but funny suggestions.
> —*Lizzy, on why she's always been an outdoor kid*

Not all the questions were for me and Jay. "What do you remember about your early adventures?" Beth and Constantine asked Molly and Lizzy. "What makes you happy on the trail?" "What have you learned to love about the outdoors?" "What do you think we should know, when we have a little girl of our own?"

"We've always loved going on trips," Molly said, skiing in no particular hurry in the middle of our little group. I grinned—her response was in character. The answer to all these questions, of course, is that it depends whom you ask, and what mood she's in when you ask her. Molly tends to have the same attitude about outdoor trips as her dad: nothing is a big deal. That epic slog? It was fun. It was "mellow." While Jay may get tense about the logistical and social details of travel (foreign currencies, complex train schedules, hordes of strangers), in our social circle he is famous (or notorious, perhaps) for his stoicism, positive attitude, and lack of drama. That thousand-mile Iditarod snow bike trip? Yeah, it was a lot of fun.

Lizzy, skiing at the front of the group, offered up more detail and more nuanced critique. With young kids, you should find trail games to play, she suggested. Keep the snacks coming. Oh, and definitely check the weather report before you go. Lizzy is perhaps a bit more like me. We're tough, sure. But if a howling gale is blowing cold rain sideways into our faces, we're likely to conclude that the adventure has begun to be . . . somewhat undesirable.

Lizzy and Molly both added, quite reasonably, that they don't actually remember the trips they took as babies. But they both—each in their own way—have plenty to say about their many adventures from preschool age on up. Some of those thoughts—and some of their distinctive voices—appear in these pages.

I'm not so new to the parenting gig any more, though I remain reluctant when giving advice. I still feel compelled to add caveats. You'll also find those sprinkled throughout this book. And you'll find some reality checks from my young co-authors and some characteristically cheerful memories from Jay. But among the four of us, we have some useful tales to tell.

Finding Motivation: Recess for Grownups

In Fairbanks, elementary schools stop allowing kids outside for recess whenever the temperature drops below -20°F (-29°C). The rule is carefully enforced, presumably for safety reasons—but that doesn't stop kids from begging adults to let them out when even that modest heat threshold is not met.

"Mom, do you think it will get up to minus twenty by recess time?" one of the twins invariably asked, as we bundled up for the morning walk to the school bus stop on particularly frigid days. Even in first grade, they understood negative numbers. They understood that minus thirty was colder than minus twenty—and they didn't want to be kept in. They weren't alone in this. All their classmates, they told me, hated indoor recess. No doubt the teachers hated it too.

Kids seem to know that the great outdoors is the place to be, even in less-than-welcoming meteorological conditions. Running, leaping, climbing, jumping, and inventing complex story-driven games are the best part of any day. Indoors is a small artificial space to which we are confined for specific purposes. Outdoors is . . . the world.

Kids get this. We adults, on the other hand, often don't. I think that has to do, to a great degree, with how we frame our activities. As my children sympathetically noted many years ago, adults don't have recess. What we do have—in one way or another—is "exercise."

Every once in a while, a friend or acquaintance will remark, wallowing in good-intentions-not-quite-realized and resolutions-foiled-by-whatever, that they ought to exercise more. Ugh, I really need to exercise more. Even if unspoken, the "ugh" is always there, wrapped up in guilt and tied with a sigh.

As Molly and Lizzy get older, they are more and more aware of this social guilt-trap. They are more and more aware of the implicit ugh. For their sake as much as for my own, I try to fight that ugh.

The word "exercise" is freighted with connotations. Out of curiosity, I typed "exercise . . . " into Google, and let Autocomplete do its magic. The first item on the dropdown list was "exercise in futility." Well, gosh.

I tried "exercise is . . . " I found that "exercise is medicine." I also learned that "exercise is good for you"—and, immediately below that, "exercise is bad for you." Finally, for those who prefer their search results wordy and directly from Public Health Reports, "exercise is a subset of physical activity that is planned, structured, and repetitive."

Planned, structured, and repetitive? Oh, science writing. I'm pretty sure I don't want to undertake anything that is "planned, structured, and repetitive." Or, if I did, I wouldn't have the strength of mind to persuade myself to do so. I have no more willpower than any of my friends do—and more likely, less.

I do, however, want to undertake "physical activity" for plenty of other reasons.

I want to get places, using simple forms of transportation that don't burn any gas, don't break down, and don't prevent me from seeing and smelling the details of the world along the way. Commuting as exercise. Shopping as exercise. Errands as exercise.

I want to roam and explore, feel the wind in my face, and find solace in solitude and wonder in wilderness. Hiking and skiing and canoeing as exercise.

I want to use my body as a tool—to lug our water, build an outhouse, and haul the wood pellets that heat our house. Life as exercise.

I want to challenge myself, pushing the limits of how far, how fast, how long I can go. I want to find the space inside myself that comes from movement and exhaustion. Adventure and racing as exercise.

Last but not least, I want to play, chasing my kids and lurching them skyward, rolling and tumbling, laughing with movement and blatant bodily fun. Joy as exercise.

I want these things, and I revel in them. Having children has encouraged me more than it has hampered me. Because, even when the thermometer reads an unpromising minus thirty, minus forty, or even minus fifty, kids understand the need for recess—not just for themselves, but for the grownups in their lives, too.

Age 0:
Precious Cargo

But How Do You Deal with . . . Baby Gear

Just the idea of lugging babies into the backwoods is daunting. A few tips—and a few judicious purchases—can make it less so. Getting outside with kids requires gear. Getting outside with kids in a climate as ludicrous as that of Fairbanks, Alaska, require . . . well, not necessarily MORE gear, but certainly DIFFERENT gear.

So, yeah, you may need to acquire some stuff. But take heart; although some items are expensive, many are not. Most can be obtained second-hand, and most can likewise be passed on to other grateful families within a few years.

Throughout this book, I've tried to mention—based on season, activity, and age of participants—what we bought, what we made, and what we never bothered with at all. No, you shouldn't head up a mountain pass in your heavy cotton blue jeans, but neither do you have to entirely outfit yourself from a high-end gear shop. When possible, I make note of the cheapest options for safety and comfort. And when I think the expensive option is really the best, I explain why I think so.

I dress to be warm, dry, comfortable, and safe. I've learned a lot, over the years, about how to stay this way—and how to make sure the kids do, too. We own a lot of fleece, wool, and nylon, and I'm happy to bore you with the details of how much of it we wear for specific activities in specific conditions. But our "exercise" clothes blur and blend with our "living our lives" clothes.

As for feeding, if you or your partner are able to nurse, keeping your infant fed is pretty darn simple: just pack more of your own favorite snacks. A lot more. Exerting yourself while feeding a baby requires a lot of calories, so go for it. You'll also want to think about timing. Before the twins were born, I had the vague notion that babies ate every three hours or so. Ha! Maybe it was because

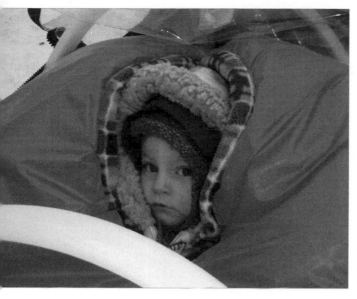

Infant and toddler winter transport included homemade sleeping bags designed to fit car seats, which were bolted into a heavy duty covered sled.
Tom Moran

they didn't get as much at each feeding, being twins, but Molly and Lizzy ate a lot more often than that. If you plan to be a supremely on-the-go family, try a carrier such as a sling that allows for relatively discreet in-motion nursing. For those who bottle-feed, powdered formula, clean water, disposable bottle liners, and spare nipples should do the trick.

Here's what you might need to obtain in order to get outdoors with babies.

Before they learn to walk, babies are luggage. Fragile luggage. Messy, loud, challenging luggage. And, of course, super-adorable and inestimably treasured luggage. But still, essentially, luggage.

The downside is the whole fragile, messy, loud, and challenging part. It's hard to overstate the complications of possessing an extraordinarily precious little duffel bag that is breakable and noisy, must be kept at a precise temperature, needs frequent liquid refueling, and insists on perpetually dampening itself.

> **TIP ▪ Baby Transport**
> One of the most expensive–but most valuable–items we purchased
> when the kids were infants was a (double) convertible bike trailer,
> ski trailer, and jogging stroller. It was a Chariot brand. We always
> referred to it as such, as if the kids were Roman Emperors, but similar
> conveyances are available from other companies. We used the Chariot
> in all three modes, and we used it pretty much daily for six years. It
> was rain-proof, bug-proof, comfortable, safe, and easy. We had to
> replace the rain cover once, when squirrels chewed through it, and
> we had to replace the tires at least twice, because we wore the tread
> right off them, but the Chariot held up remarkably well. When the kids
> finally moved on to bigger and better things, we passed along the
> Chariot to a friend. For all I know, it's out there still.

On the plus side, babies love being luggage. This is the central
tenet of the whole "baby-wearing" movement, which as far as I can
tell is not really a movement at all, but merely a reiteration of what
all parents everywhere have known forever: the baby wants to be in
motion, and the baby does not want you to put it down. So long as
you are willing to deal with hauling the extra weight and planning
for the extra complications, you can take a baby with you on everything from mundane jaunts to ambitious perambulations.

Babies enjoy strollers, joggers, bike trailers, ski trailers, and sleds.
Babies adore backpack carriers, front carriers, and slings. I'm gener-
alizing here, but my experience with my own kids is augmented by
my experience caring for my infant niece, friends' kids, babysat kids,
and the infant on a recent flight from Newark to Seattle who was
walked up and down the aisle by both parents, a helpful stranger,
and the chipper young man who was our flight attendant.

Babies tend to treat all these conveyances as Magic Sleep Inducers. During the twins' first winter, our friend and neighbor Jen had an infant, too, quite conveniently. (This child continues, conveniently, to be the same age as Molly and Lizzy, although she is no longer so conveniently located). Almost every day, Jen and I took the three babies out for a drag. That is, we wrapped them up, stuck them in sleds, and marched along the snowy trails that wind for miles through the stunted spruce trees that we call "forest." It was Enforced Locomotive Naptime. I've heard of parents doing the same thing in cars, driving laps to nowhere just to get their little Taylor or Parker to snooze. The advantage of doing this on foot is that you can feel virtuous about your low carbon footprint and your healthy outlook, while also getting a chance to stomp. I'm pretty certain that stomping is therapeutic for new parents.

In fact, babies sleep so well while in motion that you may find that you need to build in rest breaks to wake them up and get them stimulated and worn out so that they will sleep again later—like, during the night.

Babies who sleep at night are a good thing. But you already knew that.

Although we're usually on the frugal side, for carrying babies we invested in relatively high-quality gear: two front/back carriers (Ergo brand), which we mostly used for day hikes and around-town jaunts, and two heavy-duty backpack carriers (made by Sherpani), each with the capacity to carry a large toddler/preschooler, plus significant quantities of gear—because we didn't have the option of having one parent carry the kid while the other carries the stuff. The packs came with removable sun shades and rain covers, which could be draped with simple mosquito-netting covers (because, yes, Alaska has a few mosquitoes). The packs also provided stirrups, so the kids could rest their feet when we most definitely were not resting ours.

We also had a couple of hand-me-down Baby Bjorn front carriers, and a lighter-weight backpack carrier (also a freebie) without all the whistles and bells. When the twins were between about three months and two years, I often found myself using these in combination, with one kid on the front and one on the back—not for long hikes (ugh!), but for walking the dogs on our local trails, or covering any other territory where the giant double stroller was impossible. It looked pretty goofy.

If you only have one baby at a time, your needs will obviously be less. If you have triplets, you will need three packs and one really, really good friend.

Lucky Thirteen Days Old: The First Hike

When the twins were fourteen days old, I dutifully lugged them—and their two unavoidably awkward car seats—through the doors of our friendly local clinic for their two-week checkup. Our doctor is a good friend and an avid (or rabid, perhaps) outdoor enthusiast. She asked how we were all doing.

"We hiked Angel Rocks yesterday!" I told her.

She stared at me for a moment. Then she laughed.

I won't deny it; in the first months of parenting, Jay and I felt

Angel Rocks Trail Loop

Location ▪ Chena Recreation Area, east of Fairbanks.

Distance and duration ▪ Three miles round trip, one afternoon.

Locomotion ▪ Hiking, carrying infants in a Baby Bjorn front carrier and a cloth sling, and carrying gear in small daypacks.

Terrain ▪ Steep and rocky, but no technical climbing; a well-used and well-marked trail.

Weather ▪ Clear and sunny summer conditions.

Accommodations ▪ Parking area with outhouses.

The babies were thirteen days old on their first hike, a three-mile jaunt at Angel Rocks. FAMILY PHOTO

like we had something to prove. We had told ourselves—PROMISED ourselves—that we were still going to be the same people we were in the PCE (Pre-Child Era). Now we had to make that true.

We were both used to spending a lot of time in motion. By the time my double pregnancy reached full term, I was about as graceful as the Goodyear Blimp. But I still rode my bike to and from work each day, garnering stares of amusement and horror. The twins were born at the end of May, when Fairbanks is typically bursting into full-fledged summer with green ardor, fueled by the nearly twenty-four hour sunshine. It felt wrong to be sitting inside. It felt stir-crazy.

So we set off for a local trailhead with two newborns; two hand-me-down Baby Bjorn carriers; plenty of spare diapers, wipes, and itty-bitty spare clothes; a picnic; and a not-yet-fully-healed Cesarean incision.

This was, clearly, a ridiculous thing to do. Although the Angel Rocks Loop is a short hike—three miles, total—it's not without challenges, rising steeply to rocky outcrops via switch-backs. It's a great trail for novices or families with young children, but it's not, by most reasonable standards, a great trail for children who still have umbilical stumps and adults recovering from major abdominal surgery.

And yet . . . it was a wonderful day. Our friends Trusten and Margaret came along, and brought their six-year-old, Robin. She leapt and clambered from rock to rock, dashed ahead, dawdled, and explored. It was sunny. It was warm. I was only tasked with carrying one baby, meaning I was lighter than I'd been in ages.

Given that we had only thirteen days of experience as parents, we planned relatively well. One of the best things about hiking with infants is that they are simple little beings. They eat, they sleep, they poop. They generally love the sound of voices, gentle rhythmic motion, and changing scenery—even if they are so young that the scenery still looks like colored blobs of light. Although new parents are often brainwashed into believing that newborns need So Much Stuff, newborns themselves are merely convinced that they need warmth and milk.

This last part was the one thing we weren't entirely prepared for. Although the magically organized infants in parenting books nurse every three hours, my infants nursed whenever the heck they wanted, which was pretty much all the time. Perhaps in part because they'd been forced to share whatever resources my confused body could produce, inside the womb and out, they were perpetually voracious.

At home, I'd already gotten the knack of feeding twins simultaneously (and typing at the same time, in a desperate effort to complete my dissertation—because I'm not actually a good planner). However, while hiking along a trail, the best I could manage was one at a time. (I probably shouldn't even admit it, but, yes, I tried to replicate the home experience).

Thus, Jay and I juggled the two of them back and forth, back and forth. Each time one squawked, it came back to me. I discovered that nursing while wearing a Baby Bjorn is awkward and immodest at best. Other front carriers—a sling, which we had at the time, and had luckily brought along, or an Ergo, which we had not yet purchased—offer better possibilities.

And so we hiked. And our doctor laughed, but gave us a pass. And so it all began.

Russian Roulette (the Diaper Version)

The hike was going beautifully until Jay's baby exploded.

If you've ever cared for a very young, perfectly healthy, milk-fed infant, you already know where this is going. If you haven't . . . well . . . let's just say the three-month-old child Jay happened to be carrying at the time made a sudden and ominously loud series of noises that resulted in the need for a change of not only her diaper, but every item on her body, NOW.

Which Jay duly began to do.

The baby immediately started screaming.

It was September, which is, in Fairbanks, our one month of fall.

Angel Rocks to Chena Hot Springs Trail

Location ▪ Chena Recreation Area. Car or bike shuttle of about nine miles needed, (not a loop hike).

Distance and duration ▪ Eight to nine miles, about five hours.

Locomotion ▪ Hiking, carrying infants in two Baby Bjorns, and carrying gear in small daypacks.

Terrain ▪ Steep and rocky with long sections above tree line, no technical climbing; a well-used and well-marked trail, although some spots could be tricky in fog.

Weather ▪ Cool fall conditions, around 50°F with a strong breeze.

Accommodations ▪ Parking with outhouses at the start, developed hot spring resort at the end.

The highest summit of the Angel Rocks to Chena Hotsprings trail is not the best place to change a diaper on a blustery autumn day. FAMILY PHOTO

It wasn't too chilly down in the valley where the hike started. But on the exposed ridgeline that connects the Angel Rocks trail with Chena Hot Springs, temperatures were probably in the 40s, with a brisk wind. In our pre-child days, this would still have passed as summery weather. In our pre-child days, a nine-mile hike would have been "short." But now our world had changed. Times two.

More screaming.

My brain was spinning with that peculiar form of adrenal horror that occurs when your infant is crying in unfettered distress. Sure, it wasn't winter, but this was not an environment in which anyone, of any age or degree of hardiness, would prefer to be stripped naked and sponged off with a dozen or more wet wipes.

The baby kept screaming.

Our three-month-old baby certainly did not appreciate such treatment. Not one little bit. But there was no choice.

Screaming.

Jay did his best. We were, at least, armed with plenty of diapers, plenty of wipes, and several dry onesies. Jay even had a clean shirt for himself. We obviously didn't have a spare carrier, so that had to just . . . be wiped.

The baby was still screaming.

This kid was REALLY unhappy with the situation. And, anxious mother that I was, I was thinking about the worst case scenarios, all of which involved hypothermia. What happens to a hypothermic baby? Was she damaged? What if we couldn't warm her up again? Had we made a terrible mistake? What the hell were we doing on a nine-mile hike on a cold, wind-swept ridge with INFANT TWINS, for heaven's sake?

So much screaming.

I hovered next to Jay, feverishly handing him items of infant hygiene and items of clothing, and stuffing nasty rejected objects higgledy-piggledy into plastic bags, all while unbuckling the other baby, the one I was carrying, so that we could swap out the two of them.

TIP ▪ Plastic Bags

Although I'm a staunch supporter of using reusable cloth bags at the grocery store, any trip with a baby or little kid—even if it's just a trip to the grocery store—can benefit from plastic bags. Just in case. The zippered kind are great for quarantining wet, gross, smelly items away from anything else in your bag, although full-on trash bags might be needed in the most dire emergencies. Bags of various types can also be used to create portioned snacks, to serve as vapor barriers separating warm dry socks from cold wet shoes, and to keep everything dry in your pack in the rain. Bags. They are extremely light. If you don't use them, you can take them again next time.

The baby was still screaming.

Finally, *finally*—after a very long four or five minutes—the child was dry and clad. But she was so very tiny, so very vulnerable, so very much still screaming at the top of her tiny, tiny lungs.

I traded out the other baby, stuffed the shrieking one in my carrier, zipped her in, and offered her sustenance.

Like magic, things got warm and quiet.

There was no more screaming on that hike. But I can't claim that the remainder of the jaunt was entirely quiet. Miles later, when Jay and I had swapped out kids again (feeding duties still being my thing), the tiny person I happened to be carrying discovered, for the very first time, that her vocal cords, mouth, and tongue might be useful for creating something other than sheer blasts of sound. "Ma!" she announced. She tried it again. "Ma! Ma!" She bounced along against my chest. "Mamamamama." The conversation seemed a little repetitive to me after the first ten minutes, but my interlocutor seemed to be enjoying herself. "Mamamama mamamama mama!"

Babies are more resilient than you think.

But How Do You Deal with . . . Keeping Babies Warm

When I'm grocery shopping and it's forty below zero, these days I typically ask the kids to zip the lettuce and spinach into their parkas just to get from the store to the car. Lettuces are just that delicate.

Babies are like lettuces.

Not in the leafy, crunchy, $2.99-per-head sense, but in terms of their need for delicate climate control. If it's cold enough that you need to wear your salad greens, you are definitely going to need to wear your baby. Conversely, if it's hot enough to wilt your lettuce—a situation which, yes, does sometimes occur even in Fairbanks—your baby is going to need shade, a minimum of clothing, and decent

> **Tip ▪ Infant Entertainment**
> In addition to being highly portable, young babies are surprisingly easy to entertain on the trail. In fact, I've found that not only my own kids, but also other babies with whom I've spent any amount of time (notably my niece Rabiah, and my friends' daughter Robin) were less bored and fussy while being toted around, whether on a city street or in the woods, than if given toys in the confines of a house. They seemed to like the security of being carried, the lulling effects of motion, the ever-changing scenery, and the sounds of human voices. They napped happily, in any kind of carrier. So long as they were fed frequently, entertainment took care of itself.

airflow. At the intermediate temperatures that occur in a salad bowl on your kitchen counter or the crisper drawer of your fridge, you have less to worry about (although I do not recommend storing your baby in either of these places).

Dressing yourself for Fairbanks-type weather is a challenge. Dressing people for this weather when they are too young to articulate which bits are cold is daunting, even terrifying.

When babies are too young to walk and play in the snow, they can be bundled into what essentially amounts to sleeping bags. Infant snowsuits that cover hands and feet are great for kids who haven't yet figured out what hands and feet are for. These are fairly easy to find.

I sewed puffy bags made of fleece, synthetic batting, and nylon, with zippers all the way up the front, and slits in the back to accommodate the straps from the girls' car seats. Similar bags are sold commercially, although none as bombproof as what I made. We used these bags not only for car travel, but also for sled travel.

Luckily, as already noted, babies love to be lugged about in warm, enclosed spaces. While many options exist for creating such a space, the most obvious warm, enclosed space in question can be, as with a head of lettuce, the inside of your jacket.

The advantages of this option are that your baby probably adores being worn, and you already know that the space in question is exactly the right temperature (assuming you are not the walking dead or actively on fire).

The disadvantages are that 1) assuming you are using a front-carry system, you are going to have to develop some resilient back muscles; and 2) the space in question is not big enough, unless you are still wearing the jacket you wore while pregnant, and even then . . . probably nope.

The issue with your back muscles may not have an easy solution. Front-carrying a heavy object for long periods of time is just plain

Babies and toddlers stay cozy when they share a parent's body heat—and they enjoy watching the action, too.
Tom Moran

awkward. If you acquired a small human by being pregnant, you've already been working on these muscles for months—but maybe need a bit of a break now. If you're a proud parent who wasn't pregnant, your complaints may be met with eye-rolls. Either way, doing this frequently as the kid gradually gets heavier will build up your tolerance. Using a good-quality carrier designed to be ergonomically fabulous will help a lot. And wearing a backpack while front-carrying your baby actually may make you more comfortable, because it balances you out. Bonus: a backpack is way less dorky than a diaper bag.

As for that issue with the size of your jacket, you could buy a jacket extender—that is, an insulated rectangle of fabric that expands the front of your coat. They exist online, because everything exists online. Or, if you're feeling ambitious—and have a vague recollection of that seventh-grade home economics class you were forced to take—you could try whipping up a nice simple extender rectangle yourself.

First, look at the zipper on your favorite jacket. Measure how long it is, note whether it's plastic or metal, and write down what gauge it is (probably a number between six and ten, representing the width of the zipped-together teeth in millimeters). Buy another zipper just like it. Buy some fleece and nylon from the remnant bin (Special! Marked down for quick sale!). Bonus points if the fleece has ninjas or elephants on it; the nylon goes on the outside anyhow. Sew a rectangle about a foot wide (depending on how close-fitting your jacket is, and also how chunky your baby is, I guess). Your sewing can be perfect, but it can also be sloppy. Open the zipper and sew one side on each side of your Rectangle of Warmth. (Note: you have to figure out which side goes where. This is actually kind of hard to do while sleep-deprived, but I'm counting on you).

And, voila. So. Much. Style.

Five Months, Fifteen Below: Infants in Winter

"At fifteen degrees below zero, being lugged along a deeply rutted trail liberally strewn with tussocks, the babies were sound asleep. I was impressed. In their unflappability, Molly and Lizzy seemed to take after their parents."

As noted earlier, Tom Moran's newspaper write-up of Molly and Lizzy's introductory winter trip brought them a modicum of local-level fame. Judging from Tom's description, it also brought them a satisfying nap. But did it bring them joy?

My co-authors are no help to me on this one. Nobody remembers being five months old—at least, not in a conscious or verbal sort of way. If they have buried memories that have scarred them forever, that is, as they say, "outside the scope of this analysis."

Anyone who has spent any time with a five-month-old might argue the things they are capable of enjoying at that age are fairly limited: cuddles, voices, rocking, bright colors and contrasting visual stimuli, items to grab, items to

Lower Angel Creek Cabin

Location ▪ Chena River Recreation Area, east of Fairbanks.

Distance and duration ▪ Eight miles round-trip, one overnight.

Locomotion ▪ Cross-country skis, with one adult pulling a specially made covered baby sled and three dogs pulling a plastic pulk gear-sled.

Terrain ▪ Mostly flat; trail mostly well broken by earlier snowmachines and mushers, but badly rutted on this trip due to shallow early-season snow and inappropriate summer use by four-wheelers in wetlands. An upland trail has since been built to deal with this problem.

Weather ▪ About -15°F and clear.

Accommodations ▪ Basic state-owned (Department of Natural Resources) rental cabin equipped with a wood stove (wood gathered by foraging and water melted from snow).

shove in one's mouth and vigorously gum, and an all-you-can-eat breast-milk buffet. Conversely, infants are strongly opposed to being chilly, being confined to unstimulating locales when wide awake, and being denied food and/or adult attention at PRECISELY the moment they demand it. Thus, a really high-quality backwoods adventure, from the perspective of two people not yet half a year old, is one that provides everything in the first category, while avoiding everything in the second.

Right. So, how did we do?

Well, Tom's archives keep my memory honest here, and the answer is decidedly . . . mixed. While the babies' ability to travel along a bumpy trail in a sled at fifteen degrees below zero (Fahrenheit!) impressed him, and while he seemed amused by their cheerful acceptance of being included in wood-gathering and wood-cutting (while strapped to a parent's chest), his thoughts on their ability to be entertained by sitting around in a darkish and somewhat drafty, chilly cabin weren't quite so positive. According to Tom, "The infants settled down at times —they were awed into silence by the flame from the cook stove, and lulled into it by a little walk around in the sled—but they remained periodically upset through the evening." Also, they apparently kept waking up through the night.

The funny part, of course, is that so many people who actually read the article—with all its truthfulness about the fractiousness of babies—apparently thought, *cool, yeah, I totally want to do that too!*

At the time, I was bemused. But now, in retrospect, I think I have a clearer perspective. Babies cry. They wake their parents over and over again, all through the night. They get gassy. They get high-maintenance. They do all this at home. They do this on backcountry winter camping trips in the depths Alaska. All things being equal, why not choose the latter?

Age 1–2:
Large Opinions,
Small Vocabularies

But How Do You Deal with . . . Hiking with Toddlers

Toddlers are fabulous hikers, so long as you don't care whether or not you make any forward progress whatsoever. With inseam lengths approaching eleven inches, their strides have all the locomotive efficiency of galloping hedgehogs. They generally have attention spans the length of a strobe light, although they can stare at a fungus or a pellet of moose poop for minutes at a time.

Like infants, toddlers are portable. Unlike infants, they don't prefer to be treated as luggage at all times. They are also heavier than infants, and spend a higher percentage of each day awake. They are old enough to have clearly felt goals and desires, but not yet old enough to clearly articulate them. Even in relatively benign summer weather, trips with toddlers take patience. Also, mosquito netting, and twice as many diapers and changes of clothes as you think you need.

Toddlerhood is the most challenging age for keeping kids warm, because they will want to roam, but lack the body mass and sustained aerobic ability to stay warm. On the plus side, a cold kid will not generally suffer in silence. Whining, whimpering, and outright screaming are good signs that a young explorer is unhappy with the current state of thermoregulation. The downside is that in extreme conditions, there's not much leeway between "chilly" and "frostbite."

The best solution we found was to bundle chilled toddlers back into whatever cozy conveyance we'd brought along. This, of course, necessitated always bringing one along.

"Cozy" in this context means "stuffed with an old sleeping bag that contains one or more quart bottles of boiling water." These simple heat sources were then—and sometimes still are—immensely popular. And maybe not just with the kids. Who doesn't appreciate an old-fashioned hot water bottle?

Baby Steps and Infinite Patience

"Out! Out!"

"Okay, I'll let you out, but you have to REALLY walk, okay?"

I was met by the burbling agreement of a child with a vocabulary of fewer than twenty words but a very clear sense of purpose. Even at the age of one, Molly liked to do things independently. She wanted to do what the big people were doing. She wanted to WALK.

I unbuckled Molly from the Chariot—now in jogging stroller mode—and plunked her onto her unsteady little feet on the muddy trail. She promptly staggered off to investigate a puddle.

Luckily, my friend Colleen, a participant on this trip, seemed to have infinite patience for this sort of thing. Ten years later, when she had a baby of her own, I figured she was well prepared, because she'd been fine with staring at fungus with my children. She was also game for helping to trick them into forward progress. "Okay, Molly, grab our hands and we'll swing you!"

Lee's Cabin from the Eliot Highway mile 28 trailhead

Location ▪ White Mountains National Recreation area north of Fairbanks.

Distance and duration ▪ Fourteen miles round-trip, one overnight.

Locomotion ▪ Hiking, with adults pushing toddlers in a double jogging stroller or occasional front-carrying in a sling to facilitate nursing, and carrying gear in backpacks.

Terrain ▪ Mixed hills and flats; trail very wide and easy to follow, with only minor wet spots.

Weather ▪ Cool, late summer weather, about 60°F.

Accommodations ▪ Basic BLM rental cabin equipped with a wood stove (wood gathered by foraging and stream water boiled or filtered).

Hiking at the pace of a toddler requires patience. The twins were 14 months old on this hike to Lee's Cabin with a family friend. FAMILY PHOTO

I've heard now that this game may not be the best for toddlers' shoulder joints, so maybe you should avoid the level of torque that would allow for interplanetary orbit, but . . . toddlers really love being swung between two adults. It gets old for the adults, but if you want to place limits on the fun, you can teach counting at the same time: "We'll swing you TEN times, okay? Help me count them . . . "

This particular hike was a seven-miler, to Lee's Cabin in the White Mountains. The weather was good, the company was good, and the trail was good. The only challenge was the two fourteen-month-old participants.

It wasn't that the twins weren't enjoying the outdoors. It wasn't that they didn't want to be there. They just wanted what they wanted—and they wanted it the moment they wanted it.

On the plus side, they were still highly distractible. If they didn't want to be in a sling or a pack, they could be temporarily amused by handing them toys, sticks, rocks, and random pieces of vegetation.

On this seven-mile hike, the toddlers mostly rode in a jogging stroller, but they liked to stretch their legs—and arms—too. FAMILY PHOTO

Spruce needles are poky! Birch leaves are soft! Balsam poplar is slightly sticky and smells interesting! Ooh, now Mommy is singing a clapping song! It has lots of verses, and lots of clapping! It would be years before Molly and Lizzy realized that Mommy is a terrible singer.

But when these amusements paled, we had to let them out. And swing them along. And let them walk, with agonizing slowness. And, at one point, when somebody REALLY wanted to nurse, that had to happen, too—her chunky fourteen-month old body stuffed into a sling while I kept on trucking and Colleen patiently pushed the stroller.

We made it the seven miles, of course—and back again. We read picture books, shared new foods with new eaters, and snuggled together in sleeping bags large and small. The trip was slow, but I'd count it as a success, in that everyone came home happy. And, as noted, Colleen was not forever averse to having a kid of her own.

But How Do You Deal with . . .
Winter Clothes—for You and for Them

Long before I had kids, I had to figure out how to stay warm and comfortable while outdoors at ridiculous temperatures. One silver lining of dealing with minus forty is that, in comparison, temperatures just barely below zero in the Fahrenheit range seem undaunting—practically balmy. And I realized, retroactively, that I could have been much more comfortable in the not-so-cold world of my childhood and young adult years.

I was able to transfer much of what I'd learned about clothing to my kids. An important caveat, of course, is to always remember that appropriate levels of insulation depend not only on what the thermometer says, but also on how much someone is exerting himself or herself, and how much thermal mass they have. Little kids can go from red-cheeked high-energy warmth to brutally cold with terrifying speed, because they are lightweights. Even now, I have different clothing needs from my big kids because, yeah, I still weigh a lot more than they do.

The bottom line is, always be over-prepared, especially when children are involved.

Mittens and other hand coverings

Hand coverings being the first clothing gear topic is not arbitrary. In most places, chilly hands are uncomfortable. In Alaska, fingers are body parts that you might not get to keep if you don't take it seriously. When gripping ski poles, hands can be particularly vulnerable.

On a lengthy cross-country ski trip, with temperatures consistently below zero and a minimum of several hours on the trail, you face a basic choice: you can freeze your fingers off, or you can wear hand-coverings that leave with the dexterity of a two-month-old infant. Choose the latter. Giant mittens (insulated, usually with a nylon exterior) or ski-pole pogies (insulated mitts that attach directly to your poles) are your friends.

Massive mitts are, of course, pretty useless if you are trying to get car keys out of your pocket, adjust a ski binding, or add a forgotten item to your grocery list. For this reason, you may find it handy to wear thin stretchy gloves or mittens as liners underneath. Layering also helps prevent your mittens from getting sweaty. Wet mittens can be a disaster in the long run. Thus, if exercise starts making your hands hot, remove a mitten-layer immediately.

For emergency purposes, it's a good idea to bring along a few sets of chemical hand-warmers, but don't rely on them too heavily. During rare moments when you really, really need to do some fine-motor task too delicate to be accomplished in any sort of gloves your only option is to take off your hand coverings for as short a time as possible. But be careful. Frostbite can happen quickly, and cold hands are painful and difficult to rewarm.

Facing the Truth

Put simply, when it gets cold enough, uncovered faces freeze. But what kind of face covering is best? There's no right answer to this question. Available options offer either direct coverage (putting some kind of fabric against the skin, as with a balaclava) or indirect coverage (creating a bubble of breath-warmed air near the face, as with a fur ruff around a deep hood).

Some people prefer neoprene ski masks, and a friend of mine even sews and sells something she calls a "nose hat." The twins and I opt for neck warmers—simple tubes of stretchy fleece that can be pulled up almost to the eyeballs, if needed. They get frosty, but they are breathable, and create enough of a warm-air envelope to keep us—thus far, at least—from losing any skin. They are also about the simplest sewing project imaginable, and can thus double as a craft activity for any age above four.

Hats Off to You

Keeping your head warm is cheap. It's also easy. Oddly, it's often neglected.

In my experience, hats are like seatbelts. You need to have one that is comfortable so that you'll actually wear it—but even if it isn't comfortable, wear it anyhow.

The most practical hats are close-fitting and lack pom-poms or other fancy bits, but if your kid adores the hat with the ears or the googly eyes, fine, go for it. The point is getting your kid to wear a hat.

Of course, the above assumes that the child is old enough to be allowed to have opinions. If your baby is old enough to yank a hat off, but not old enough to untie knots or understand logic, get something with as dorky a chinstrap as possible, and enforce the hatting.

Wool hats tend to be itchy; fleece is comfier, but neither is particularly wind resistant. I don't find this to be a problem, because when it's really cold, I pull my hood over my hat.

Wait . . . you do have a hood, right? A jacket without a good hood—meaning a hood that is insulated, fits closely but not tightly over a decent hat, and closes all the way up to your chin—is as ridiculous as a good hood without the jacket.

Under Where?

Long underwear is so, so cozy. Sporty long underwear—meaning the non-cotton kind, sold at outdoor stores and even at some cheaper retailers—also wicks away sweat and prevents you feeling clammy and dangerously chilled when you stop sweating. One downside is that there is no way to remove long underwear politely and quickly. If you are likely to become rapidly overheated in indoor spaces, you won't want to wear your thermals all winter long. But for any sort of outdoor adventure, it can't be beat. As soon as the kids were old enough to hike, bike, and ski, we bought them good-quality long johns, just like ours (but maybe a few sizes smaller).

Sensitive Subjects

Given that I am female, and my juvenile advisors are likewise girls, I'm not entirely qualified to give advice about keeping external genitalia warm. However, on behalf of those who may face this important concern, I'll mention that outdoor retailers market briefs with wind-proof front panels.

If you're a long way out on a chilly trail and haven't planned properly, interposing a spare sock, mitten, hat, or neck warmer into the crucial region will solve the problem—or so I hear.

You're welcome, guys.

The Outer Layer

Although one might imagine that at the insanely cold temperatures on offer in Fairbanks, I'd wear an enormous jacket six months of the year, I rarely do.

Puffy parkas are for when you stop moving. I carry a compressible one—synthetic, in my case, although down is great too—on all jaunts. It's hooded and cozy, and big enough to fit over all my other layers. But I don't put it on much.

When in motion, I dress in layers: long underwear, fleece, all the attention to appendages already mentioned, and then a relatively thin windproof but somewhat breathable layer on top.

I've had the same pair of slightly stretchy windproof pants for fifteen years. They're still just fine, except for a small scorch mark from that time I stood too close to a wood stove. I bought them overlarge, and when it's truly frigid, I wear long johns and fleece pants underneath.

TIP ▪ Toddler Games

Unlike infants, toddlers no longer consider the sound of your voice and the blur of passing trees to be adequate entertainment. One- and two-year-olds want games, songs, and exciting opportunities for discovery.

Unfortunately, games that this age group find entertaining are often brain-meltingly dull or straight-up alarming to adults. "Name the Thing" and "Point to the Thing" are favorites, along with "Bang on the Thing," "Carry the Thing Around," and "Try to Eat the Thing."

On the plus side, I found such games no worse on the trail than at home, at the grocery store, or anywhere else. And toddlers really do love lots of quality time with their parents. Their "conversations" might seem limited, but I was often amazed by how much they understood of my own story-telling and chatter, and how fast they were able to learn new words. Plus, toddlers are under the assumption that you are good at singing, are totally-not just making up random words to the song, know the correct answer to all questions, and are infinitely wise. Hold onto this as long as you can.

At the very least, if you're in a place you love, doing something you enjoy, your kids will pick up on that. Win.

My favorite jacket is likewise old, comfortable, and practical. It had a hood that fits well, and it's big enough to fit over a long underwear top and a fleece jacket, but not so big that it bags and flaps around me.

Warm toes

Wool socks come in many brands, some of them so high-tech that I need to get out my reading glasses to peruse the labels. Truth be told, they all seem pretty good to me. If you are going for a particularly long jaunt, or if your feet—or your kid's feet—are prone to chafing, blistering, or sweating, I'd recommend using thin moisture-wicking synthetic sock liners under the wool. It's like long underwear for feet.

Wool socks are much more expensive than cotton socks, but there's simply no choice on this issue. Save the cheaper cotton socks for May through September—unless you are wearing sandals. If you are wearing cotton socks with sandals, I probably can't help you.

Slip-Sliding Away

If you are just getting going on cross-country skis, there's no need to invest in a brand new setup. In Fairbanks and other outdoorsy communities, there are regular "gear swaps" each fall, at which you can find used skis, poles, and boots. Online gear sales are also an option. Kids' skis are handed down from family to family.

For classic skiing, poles should stand just below shoulder height. Skis should be flexible enough that if you put all your weight on one ski on a flat smooth floor, it touches the ground under your foot—but rigid enough that when you distribute your weight between both skis, there's a no-touch zone. This is the area where you will apply kick-wax.

Your ski boots—and your kids' ski boots—should have the same type of bindings as their respective skis. They should fit with a little room to spare. That's it. You're ready to go

Well-bundled toddlers can still move with surprising speed.
Family Photo

Little "Helpers"

"Sure, Robin, you can take a turn with the saw."

There are few things more appealing to an eight-year-old than being allowed to help, especially if it involves sharp tools. And there's no problem with giving sharp tools to your friends' eight-year-old, so long as they are very good friends.

Alaska's backwoods cabins, on both federal (Bureau of Land Management) and state (Alaska Department of Natural Resources) land are rustic, appealing, and cozy—so long as you keep the wood stoves fed. Gathering dead wood is not a terrible chore, but it can take a bit of time to get it all sawed to stove-length with a hand-held bow-saw.

Robin fell to her task with enthusiasm and inefficiency. Sawing takes practice, and after a couple of laborious cuts, I could see she was ready for a different job. "How about I saw some wood, and you stack it?"

It didn't surprise me that Robin agreed. She was a reasonably helpful child, and she adored being outside on any pretext. And it certainly shouldn't have surprised me that once Robin was hard

---

Eleazar's Cabin from the Eliot Highway mile 28 trailhead

Location ■ White Mountains National Recreation area, north of Fairbanks.

Distance and duration ■ Twenty-six miles round-trip, one overnight.

Locomotion ■ Skiing, three dogs pulling a specially built sled with two toddlers in it, an eight-year-old skijoring behind it. Snowmachine to haul most gear.

Terrain ■ Mixed hills and flats with a long hill at the end; trail very wide and easy to follow, with good snow cover.

Weather ■ Very late winter, with nightly lows well below freezing, but highs of about 40°F and clear sunshine.

Accommodations ■ Basic BLM rental cabin with a wood stove (wood gathered by foraging and water melted from snow).

Even the youngest kids like to help, as demonstrated by this dedicated firewood crew (age 21 months) at Eleazar's Cabin. FAMILY PHOTO

at work, Molly, then aged twenty-one months, wanted in on the log-hauling action.

"Me too!"

Lizzy seemed to think that maybe the smaller kindling looked more manageable. But she wasn't going to be left out of the action.

Although there was still snow on the ground— this was a ski trip, which had made hauling the twins in by sled-dog-power quick and easy—temperatures were mild. This was what passes for spring in Fairbanks. Still, the twins were wearing snowsuits, which made them look even more rotund and ungainly than they really were. Their legs were short. Their arms were shorter. Their lifting power was limited, to say the least. But they wanted to stack wood? Well, heck yes, let them stack wood!

I sawed. Robin sawed. Robin's parents showed up with more dead wood. Jay got the wood stove crackling. And the twins stacked wood. One or two small pieces at a time, back and forth, with great care and greater earnestness.

It probably took them an hour to get everything stacked to their satisfaction. I could have made the same pile in five minutes. But that, of course, was not the point.

Me help too!

But How Do You Deal with . . . Looooong Winters

"Look! The leaves are falling!" The toddlers, having no idea that this was not a unique occurrence, were thrilled. Yellow birch leaves adorned every hillside, and the willows had turned every Crayola shade between burnt umber, tangerine, and crimson. The mornings were lightly frosted, but by nine a.m. the sun had burnt away the chill and promised an afternoon of playgrounds and bike riding. September in Fairbanks is beyond reproach. And yet, every year, I found myself fighting a mental battle against the fading fireweed and yellowing leaves.

This doesn't exactly qualify as an idiosyncrasy. Fairbanks in autumn is full of people desperately trying to insulate partially-built homes, persuade tomatoes to ripen before they freeze, and split eight gazillion cords of firewood. Railing against the onset of fall is so common that it didn't occur to me that I needed to justify it—until Jay and the kids challenged my view of reality.

Winter, Jay maintained—honestly perplexed that anyone might think otherwise—has a lot to offer. There was so much cross-country skiing and snow-biking to be done! There were miles of perfect trails right outside our doors. There were winter races, and trips to remote cabins!

And the kids? Like all children, they lived in the moment. Yellow leaves? Yay, leaves! Snow? Yay, snow!

They were right, of course. I knew that I enjoyed all these things too. And even during the extreme depths of January, I could easily cast my mind forward to sometime around Valentine's Day, when rapidly returning sunshine glitters on the snow, the ice park offers small children exhilarating ways to injure themselves, and the ski trails are sheer perfection. March in Fairbanks may be one of Alaska's best kept secrets. Don't let anyone know how nice it is, or we'll be mobbed by curious visitors.

Every day I put on snowpants first–very important, the first part–hopefully after peeing. They have to be hauled over my regular cargo pants, making me look really fat. Don't worry, you'll look just as large when you put on heavy-duty pants, too. Then my jacket. I'm pretty sure it has been passed down from my neighbor, Jacq, then my sister, then to me. Next I usually shove a wool hat below a hood, sometimes with a fleece neck gaiter, too. Now here I always make the mistake: boots BEFORE mittens. Once you have the giant gloves on, your fingers don't work for doing any small tasks. The mittens have to go off again to pull the snowpants' gaiters over your boot. I have these boots that look like I could use them in Antarctica. I get some weird looks. But truthfully, my desire to be warm overrules my desire to be fashionable, as my friends hopelessly try to warm toes inside sheepskin Uggs. I guess I've heard too many stories about my dad's friend frostbiting his feet.

Mom holds the phone talking to Grandma when we play outside. We are saving time as we walk up the driveway by doing the phone call then. "Hey, Gram, I'm ankle deep in snow! Now it's up to my knees! And now I've hopped into the snowbank, and I'm swimming in fluff!" Grandma is horrified we might get cold. All I feel is my down jacket.

–Lizzy, describing the "normal" process of dressing

Other seasons are pretty high on the awesomeness scale, too. The fantastic March fun lasts well into April. Hard on its heels, May is like a can of sweetened condensed spring: in the space of thirty-one days, we go from slush puddles and bare branches to a lush green wonderland generously splashed with the red-pink of wild roses. Little reindeer calves stagger about on wobbly legs. Everyone finds all the possessions they lost under the snow seven months previously. By the end of the month, it's summer.

Summers are great in interior Alaska: warm and sunny enough for sand castles, drippy ice cream cones, and free Vitamin D, but almost never so hot to make me long for air conditioning, ice packs, or a ticket to Antarctica. Between June and August we get everything we should—shorts, bike rides, lakeshores, butterflies, berry picking—with a few mosquitoes thrown in to remind us that life isn't perfect.

Nonetheless, when I mentally reviewed the full wheel of our seasons, I knew I didn't really want perpetual July. Plenty of people yearn for a climate in which halter tops are year-round garb, but I've never been one of them. I spent more than two years living in sunny Jamaica, and I know that unrelenting heat makes me wilt with sweat and boredom. I missed the sensation of sleeping snuggled under a blanket. I wanted to eat steaming bowls of soup and drink mugs of cocoa. I wanted to welcome—rather than resent—having a cat curl up in my lap. I want winter.

Winter here starts in October, when the muddy trails freeze firm and the first flying snowflakes bring back my own memories of being a kid in the suburbs of New York. Back then, at the first sign of dark gray winter clouds, I'd rush to tap the barometer and comb through the meteorological predictions. "It's snowing, it's snowing!" Radiators draped with sodden mittens were evidence of joy and contentment. Even if the grownups felt otherwise, I hated the fact that in the greater New York area, snow turns to brown sludge and disappears within days.

Fairbanks snow doesn't disappear. Here, November and December offer the sort of non-denominational picture-book holiday season that always seemed frustratingly elusive to me as a child. Sleigh bells? Sure, just hang some on the dog sled. Jack Frost? Yup. Chestnuts roasting on an open fire? Maybe a wood stove, but close enough. White Yuletides are guaranteed. The winter solstice is imbued with deep meaning for everyone, not just meteorologists and Wiccans. Our property is almost entirely vegetated by Christmas trees. Every year, we take forever wading through drifts, hemming and hawing and debating until we select one that is JUST RIGHT. My daily commute takes me past enough reindeer for Santa to field a full team, plus substitutes. December in Fairbanks is delightful.

Then the New Year arrives with a thud. The holidays are over. It is still woefully cold and dark, and the end is not in sight. Into January, the weather is not just harsh, it's downright mean. There's cold, and there's nose-hair-crackling cold, and then there's the sort of cold that makes any inch of exposed flesh try to turn itself inside out. A little boy at the twins' preschool lost a substantial amount of tongue to the iron railing next to the playground steps. I always thought this was something that occurred only in fiction, but a long-suffering preschool teacher assured me that in Fairbanks, it passes for normal. She's thawed dozens of tongues.

What I realized I was dreading, then, was not winter, but the season called January. January in Fairbanks is much too long. It's at least thirty-one days too long—and usually more. The groundhog doesn't even bother to check for his shadow around here; he leaves our entire ecosystem to his hardier marmot cousins. Thus, belying math and logic, January is sometimes up to sixty days too long.

Knowing this didn't really change anything, of course, but at the same time it changed everything. It solved half my problem in a single slice of logic. I, too, could live like a kid: in the moment.

It's not January now, I told myself. It's only September, and I love September! If I behaved the way dogs and kids do, I could enjoy all the terrific seasons while they were happening, without having to mope about what I'm losing or what comes next.

And when January did arrive, as it has continued to do with distressing regularity, I've used a multi-pronged strategy to deal with it, based on well-tested Fairbanks traditions. The first approach is creating an alternate reality in which we hang out in over-heated fluorescent-lit buildings wearing t-shirts and eating ice cream. The second coping mechanism? Boasting. Yes, Fairbanksans do this. It involves posting weather reports to Facebook in order to prove that we are suffering more than anyone in Maine or Idaho or Saskatchewan, and are therefore superior, albeit in a fraternity-hazing-ritual kind of way. And the final option? That involves bundling up in so many clothes that we can be rolled around like beach balls, and pretending that we're enjoying long jaunts by headlamp. Ah, family. We love January.

Age 3–4:
Short Legs,
Short Attention Spans

Getting Out the Door with Preschoolers

I think there should be a special branch of philosophy dedicated to the art of patiently waiting for twin preschoolers to get dressed to play outside . . . in Fairbanks Alaska . . . in January. We could call it The Zen of Attention Deficit Snowpants.

I distinctly recall overhearing a conversation between my mother and father when I was eight, in which they bemoaned my seeming inability to bring home from school things like permissions slips, assignments, lunch boxes, and sometimes my own head. They simply couldn't fathom why my brain sometimes escaped from orbit and headed for Neptune. And then I became a parent, and hit payback time.

For what seemed like many years, I orchestrated outdoor adventures with small people who couldn't remember that after putting on the LEFT boot, it is almost always going to be necessary to put on the RIGHT boot too.

"Ok, honey, you need to focus on finding your mitten right now . . . where do you think you left it?" I'm not sure why I bothered to ask questions like this, because the answer was always the same: "I don't know." This was all the more frustrating because I knew I was at least partly to blame. The twins were four. I was thirty-eight. If

From age three to four, we were already hot on the trails. My advice for hiking with tiny kids is keep them motivated. Bring lots of perfectly disgustingly unhealthy snacks. On trips I could eat foods that I was never allowed to eat at other times, which made trips special for me. We always played entertaining games (to a three-year-old) like "Name a word that starts with the letter on the cookie". My opinion is, teach kids that going outside is fun, then there'll be no, 'Are we done yet?'
–Lizzy, on inspiring the youngest outdoorspeople

Mommy had been focusing, Mommy would know where the mitten was. But I was busy focusing on the bag of snacks, the water bottles, the sack of overdue library books, the car keys, and my wallet, not to mention my own boots, hat, mittens, sweater, jacket, and neck warmer.

At long last, the kids made it to the doormat, and the dressing began. I stood by to dispense basic rules of physics (the snowpants have to go on BEFORE the jacket), and to help maintain focus. "Lizzy, you don't really need to bring Kanga. Okay, Lizzy, you can bring Kanga, but can you also please choose a hat? Lizzy, please choose a hat. Lizzy? Hat? HAT! HAT! HAT!"

Heaven help us if it was a "real" winter day, because at minus forty, each kid needed a balaclava, a neck warmer, AND a hat. That's after we'd already dealt with the two pairs of socks, the long underwear, and the extra sweater, and before we broached the snowpants, jacket, boots, two pairs of mittens, and head lamp.

We did, eventually, make it out the door. We waddled down the path. Just as we were approaching the car, someone remembered: we left Kanga sitting on the mat.

This was the point in time at which I needed to perfect the deep breathing techniques of the Zen of Attention Deficit Snowpants. Hyperventilating inside a balaclava is a bad idea, and yelling has been proven, through repeated not-at-all-scientific trials, to be counterproductive. But, perhaps even more importantly, I needed to be calm so I could think this through, and I needed to think this through so I could decide whether I should worry, laugh, or move to Barbados.

There isn't much margin for error in a climate as harsh as ours, and there are things that simply Cannot Be Forgotten. Luckily, not everything falls into that category. We all—not just the four-year-olds among us—have limited focus. Thus, it helps to remember that there can be joy amidst anarchy. There can be contentment in the face of distraction. There can be humor in that moment when you open the trunk of the car and realize that something is utterly, irrevocably missing. All of us can strive to attain the level of peace and harmony epitomized by The Zen of Attention Deficit Snowpants.

Backseat Driver in Your Backpack Carrier

"Daddy, you should use your map!"

The fog was so dense that Lizzy was a ghostly form, tucked into Jay's kid-carrier amid strapped-on stuff-sacks, equally indistinct. She sounded both worried and chiding—somewhere between cranky toddler and concerned grandma. Behind us, the nearest cairn was rapidly disappearing, although we'd left it only moments before. The next one was likely to more than a couple of hundred feet ahead of us—the Chena Dome Trail is well marked above tree line by these piles of stones—but it might as well have been miles.

"Yeah, use your map! Like Dora the Explorer!" agreed Molly, thirty-five pounds of

Chena Dome Trail loop

Location ■ Chena River Recreation Area, east of Fairbanks.

Distance and duration ■ ~30 miles, three days and two nights.

Locomotion ■ Hiking, with kids walking about half the time, and at other times riding in Sherpani kid-carrier packs loaded with all our gear.

Terrain ■ Very hilly, although never technical; trail well marked, but extremely hard to follow above tree line in fog.

Weather ■ Very cool and foggy summer weather, about 50°F with almost no visibility.

Accommodations ■ Parking area at trailhead, one trail shelter with water collection, but water can be limited on this hike. Tent camping only

The 29-mile Chena Dome Trail affords spectacular views on a clear day.
FAMILY PHOTO

useless but characteristically cheerful advice on my own back. The trash-bag-swathed roll of our four foam sleeping pads, ultra-light but gargantuan, made my pack appear to be something out of the labors of Hercules.

If your idea of a good hike involves covering more than five miles in a day, the preschool years are the hardest time to pull that off. Three and four-year-olds adore hiking, but their legs are still chubby, stubby little things that swing along at a brisk striding pace of one mile per hour. They are full of energy and excitement, but both those qualities tend to plummet at about 1 p.m., also known as nap time. Even if your kids no longer nap regularly at home, there's nothing like a morning of constant motion and backwoods thrills to make eyelids droop and tempers fray post-lunch. I mean, be honest, wouldn't you enjoy an afternoon nap during a long hike?

I remember about five things from our bike trip around Ireland when I was three. First, making a fence for the stuffed animal, Lambie. Second, telling a cheerful pedestrian that my favorite thing about the trip was the imaginary polar bears. Third, ponies. Fourth, I did not get the scenic bike seat, probably due to the fact that I was undersized for the weight minimum. And fifth, throwing spaghetti sauce at Dad. It's funny how none of these things I remember have anything to do with actually doing any work.

–Lizzy, reflecting on what impresses small children

Jay and I addressed the shortcomings of preschoolers by entering a phase of advanced partial lugging. In other words, we planned ambitious hikes—ten hilly miles per day—but only counted on the kids completing half that distance, in the morning. Come the post-noon hours, we sucked it up and increased the weight of our packs—still our Sherpani kid-carriers—by as much as 35 pounds. The twins napped. We trudged. If we hadn't reached our destination by the time they woke, they got out and trotted along for a bit longer.

Now, the kids were very much awake—but it was a tricky time for walking, for any of us. Patiently, Jay and I tried to explain to our preschoolers that there are a few crucial differences between the picture-book universe and the grim white-out we were now inhabiting. Even Dora herself could not make use of a paper map in dense fog—not even if she counted to ten in Spanish.

At this age, we encouraged the kids to walk as much as they could, and offered lots of snacks and praise and entertainment (How many blue things can you name? Can you spy something that starts with D, a duh sound? Can we make up new verses to 'If You're Happy and You Know It'? You can? Rock on!). However, we tried not to make them feel bad about getting tired and needing a break—because even if thirty-five pounds feels awfully heavy when added to an already bulging load, thirty-five pounds is still a very tiny human being.

This sort of heavy lifting might not seem doable, desirable, or even remotely sane to many. If the idea of compressing your vertebrae is unappealing, there are still plenty of outdoor options for conveyances easier on the spine, such as heavy-duty jogging strollers, canoes, bike trailers, and sleds.

But sometimes the problem isn't the conveyance, it's the conditions. "Mama! It's wet! Can't see!"

Hiking in dense fog is bleak. It's cold. It's disorienting. It's boring. It's slow. In short, it sucks. It was at about this point that I started singing. Thereafter, I was not permitted to stop. Like, ever. How many child-pleasing songs do you know? More than one verse? On key? Yeah, neither did I.

At the time, we didn't know whether the twins would remember anything about these trips. I'll let them settle the score on that question.

At four years old, the twins were enamored with finding each of the 28 numbered mile markers on the Chena Dome Trail. FAMILY PHOTO

You Don't Have to Be a Superhero
to be Your Kids' Superhero

"I love my mommy because she rides us to school in a Chariot." This Mother's Day proclamation from 2010 was laminated for posterity by the ever patient and good-humored teachers at Bunnell House Preschool.

That card not only advertised the fact that through those years I hauled the kids about in a nifty convertible trailer with a lofty Greco-Roman-sounding name, but also featured a drawing of me doing some sort of peculiar-looking calisthenics. I'm stretching all four limbs—each adorned with precisely five distinct digits. Whatever I'm doing must be fun, because I have an enormous blue smile on my egg-shaped head. Egg-head or not, though, the message seems unambiguous: Mommy is all about brawn, not brains.

I tacked this masterpiece up in my office, because I have a deep-seated appreciation for Crayola as an artistic medium. The work was created with the greatest goodwill on the part of Molly the young artist. Still, at the time the card slightly discomfited me. As I sat at my computer, peering at an array of downscaled Global Circulation Model data or enjoying literary treats like "Development of scale-free climate data for western Canada" and "A high resolution bioclimate map of the world," I wondered whether my kids had the right idea about who Mommy was, exactly. Then I wondered whether I did, too.

It seemed ironic to me—and disingenuous—to be labeled as the mom who bikes or jogs everywhere. With embarrassing regularity, I met strangers who said, "You're the one who runs with your kids!"

From our point of view, our system was great—quick, efficient, and consistent. I didn't have to plug in and preheat a car, I didn't have to jockey for parking, and I got my circulation and my brain going. We live about three miles from the preschool, which is also conveniently just half a mile from my office. For the sake of safety, the trailer was covered in reflectors and boasted no less than three red blinking lights. But I think passing strangers were sometimes horrified. Once, a woman actually pulled over, at thirty below zero, to ask me if I really had babies back there.

> I remember every day when we were going to preschool our mom would put boiling water in Nalgene water bottles and give them to us in the back of our Chariot, along with a sleeping bag. We also ate breakfast in the Chariot, so it had a bunch of crumbs from the cereal we ate out of plastic bags.
> –Molly, on the comforts of winter biking as a toddler

"Are you two okay back there?" I called to the kids.

"Yes, Mommy!" they replied.

Their response was perfectly audible and convincing. They WERE fine. But Concerned Lady still looked deeply dubious, and I still spent the rest of the day worrying about what the world thought of my parenting techniques.

Some people seem to find my antics on bikes and skis commendable, while others clearly think I'm only a few blue tarps away from the lunatic fringe. Either way, they have typecast me as a dedicated athlete. This is laughable. "I'm not a jock!" I want to tell them. "I'm a nerd!"

I don't mean that pejoratively. I've always been a nerd. I'm used to it, and it fits me comfortably. I was the toddler who sat at a green plastic desk, playing the role of earnest pupil, while my big sister Sarah taught me everything she'd learned at school. I was the kid who looked forward to Mathletes meets, entered every contest in the Summer Reading Program, and as a kindergartener sent a letter to Kellogg's, complaining about their misspelling of "Krispy."

When the kids got a break from exertion on the Chilkoot Trail, the parents definitely did not. FAMILY PHOTO

Sports, on the other hand, were not my strong point. I swung a bat without any apparent regard for the location of the ball. Roller-skating at early-eighties birthday parties, I clung to the walls. The only time I made contact with the ball in flag football was when it slammed me directly in the nose.

I suppose in the back of my mind, I assumed my kids would take the same trajectory I did, learning to read years before learning to ride a bike. Thus, I felt a peculiar mix of surprise, pride, and alarm when Molly and Lizzy did the opposite. They became avid fans of not only the Chariot, but our single and double tag-along bikes and their own miniature two-wheelers too. They wove among innocent bystanders on local footpaths fast enough to cause their daddy to panic.

Nerd that I am, I found myself wondering if perhaps the kids weren't gaining skills in the "optimal" order. I wondered whether, by all my hiking, biking, ski racing, and running, I was serving as a role model for brawn over brains.

Luckily, all that biking and running also gave me plenty of time for corralling my straying thoughts into some semblance of logic. Does it really matter in what order they learn, so long as they are having fun, and just being happy kids?

Spoiler alert: they learned to read. The passage of time eases many an anxiety.

Molly and Lizzy are now avid about reading AND riding bikes—although not, I hope, at the same time. They ask me questions such as "Is peanut butter a Newtonian solid?" and "What causes radioactive decay?"

Maybe now I've got what I wanted all along. I can be a scientist AND a representative for non-motorized transportation. Maybe one day my kids will be able to look back and appreciate me for an eclectic range of attributes and activities.

These days, I'm happy to see bicycles stacked up in the bike shed, math competition paperwork stacked on the end table, and library books jammed into the corners of beds. With nostalgia and hindsight, I'm thrilled that Molly was proud of me, even if only for my brute-force pedal power.

Lizzy's Mother's Day card is displayed on my wall, too.

"I love that Mommy can still pick us up," it says.

But How Do You Deal with . . . Packing Light

In the struggle to keep moving while weighted down with two growing kids and all their accoutrements, Jay and I became experts in hiking and camping light—particularly when sleds, wheels, or boats weren't helping with the burden.

In part, this meant simply limiting what we took along. Lots of books and websites offer tips on how to do this, but a here are a few basics that we learned along the way:

Take one light cooking pot, and use it only to heat water. Our dinners tend to be relatively wholesome, within the limits of ultra-light camping cuisine. While you can purchase just-add-water camping meals in foil pouches, we find these a bit expensive and limited. We generally opt to base our meals off an instant starch (minute rice, powdered potatoes, couscous) and add a range of dried veggies, seasonings, fats, and proteins, such as various tasty

So, you might think, "People in Alaska must have really expensive clothes and jackets to stay warm!" Today, I'm going to share the merits of hand-me-downs. When you buy a coat, it is always not quite as warm as it should be, not as nice as it could be, and not as many pockets as you could possibly want. The jackets you want are usually $600 new. When kids think, "hand-me-downs", they groan, and probably don't think of hand-me-downs as sometimes a benefit. However, when you go to a second-hand store, you can usually find a perfect coat for maybe fifty bucks. I look at my own coat. It has been passed down from Jacq to Molly and from Molly to me. Now, it's a kids' coat. New, I think the price was around $300. Here we do the opposite of what you might think. To get a coat that's warm and has an optimal number of storage pockets, everyone's glad for the hand-me-downs.

–Lizzy, suggesting ways to economize on gear

TIP ▪ Small Sleeping Bags

You might be tempted to use an adult bag for your kid, based on the fact that high-quality light-weight full-size bags are easier to find, more likely to be available on sale or second-hand, and unlikely to be outgrown. But kids can get very cold with too much air space around them, and their small body mass makes it hard for them to retain heat. Get an extra-warm bag that's the right size. When you're done with it, you can pass it on so some other lucky little adventurer.

---

cheeses and nuts. Molly and I are vegetarian, but hard sausages or jerky are options for the omnivores.

Select lightweight synthetic clothing, wool, and down clothing that can be layered—for safety and comfort, as well as for weight. Take one change of clothes for the kids, in case things get wet—but that's it. Just get dirty.

Do bring some toys, if you are on a long jaunt, but pare it down to a few ounces— e.g., one stuffed animal, an Uno deck, and half a dozen of the paper storybooks that conveniently often come free in Cheerios boxes.

Invest in key items of ultra-light gear. Tiny inexpensive stoves that screw directly into small propane cylinders are great, like the Pocket Rocket. Old-school foam sleeping pads such as the RidgeRest are super-light, and fairly cheap, albeit bulky.

The priciest items on our gear list have included ultra-light sleeping bags and tents. They were worth it—we've gotten a ton of use out of them. We used a three-person featherweight tent until the kids were six, and put them feet to feet on one pad. Now we have a five-person pyramid tent with a single pole in the center. It's spacious and comfortable.

A caveat: with all your gear, be sure you know how it works. In our continuing efforts to use the most efficient and lightweight camping gear available, Jay purchased a cooking pot with a special heat-distributing base. It did, indeed, boil water faster. Alas, what I didn't realize, when I first put it on our roaring little stove, was that the corrugated bottom was protected by a plastic cover. For the remainder of the trip, we were picking bits of melted plastic out of our stove. None of my family members will ever let me forget this.

When the kids grew older and taller, we upgraded to a spacious ultra-light pyramid-style tent. We love it—but in windy locations, placing large rocks on the tent stakes is crucial. FAMILY PHOTO

"Klondike Ho!"—Multi-Day Backpacking, Preschool Style

A motley assortment of camping stoves roared and hissed in the open-sided shelter overlooking the lake. Just-add-water cuisine was clearly the order of the evening, as each group concocted steaming sacks of freeze-dried sustenance. Colorful bags optimistically advertised their contents: chicken a la king, pasta primavera, beef stroganoff. A few clouds had rolled in, and it was starting to drizzle. Almost all the hikers were huddled on the wooden benches. Some of them looked distinctly foot-sore.

Lizzy and Molly were jumping. "D'you see the red lights?" Molly demanded, pointing to her sneakers. "See? They blink!"

I was hovering nearby, ready to employ diversionary tactics ("Gosh, kids, let's go look for bugs under rocks!") if any of our fellow hikers seemed less than thrilled by my offspring. However, the middle-aged man from Montana had time to kill while his stomach

The Chilkoot Trail

Location ▪ Klondike National Park, out of Skagway.

Distance and duration ▪ 33 miles, five days and four nights.

Locomotion ▪ Hiking, with kids walking most of the time, and at other times riding in Sherpani kid-carrier packs loaded with all our gear.

Terrain ▪ Extremely varied, from coastal rainforest to above tree line; extremely steep over the pass, although never technical; trail well marked and heavily used.

Weather ▪ Varied, from cool rain around 50°F to sunny at about 70°F.

Accommodations ▪ Designated campsites that must be reserved in advance, and include tent platforms, cooking areas, drinking water, and outhouses. Some interpretive signs and rangers on the trail. Train available from the end of the hike back to Skagway.

The massive trees of Alaska's coastal rainforest were a novelty to children from the state's sub-Arctic interior. FAMILY PHOTO

rumbled. His own teenage kids were busy preparing something starchy and beige. He smiled, and duly admired Molly's shoes. "Did you hike over the pass wearing those?" he asked.

I winced a little at the question, and tried to judge whether Montana Guy was more amused than downright horrified by such a flagrant violation of the National Park Service's Appropriate Gear List. I'd considered trying to obtain miniature hiking boots, but the possibility of blisters in new footwear had seemed even more likely than the chance that third-hand playground-wear might simply disintegrate atop a rocky precipice.

"These are my Thomas the Tank Engine sneakers," said Molly, as if that explained everything. "The old ones with Spiderman were too little. These ones are size ten!"

Toddler tens—my kid was practically Sasquatch.

Since long before we even set out on the Chilkoot Trail—in fact, ever since Jay and I first casually mentioned our plans for our end-of-summer family trip—I'd seen eyebrows skyrocketing. Were we sure it was really wise? How could we cover thirty-three miles of rough terrain with twin four-year-olds, carrying all our own gear, and all their gear—including the requisite stuffed animals, bedtime stories, and footy pajamas? What about gale force winds, mud, bugs, and unceasing rain? What about bears? What about the notorious Chilkoot Pass, which had tortured

> I really clearly remember standing on a narrow ledged trail, and I was on the inside. A group of hikers went past, and I stamped my foot, demanding that they look at my blinky Thomas the tank engine shoes.
> –Molly, recalling what empowers a four-year-old

even the grizzly-looking miners of the Yukon Gold Rush? And that was the reaction from our friends. Once we were on the trail, strangers outright stared. "You're not going the whole way, are you?"

I pointed out that, as on other hikes, we planned to carry the kids in backpack carriers for almost half the distance, usually encompassing post-lunch nap time. This wasn't taken as an effective comeback. It seemed our questioners lacked faith in the ability of a thirty-something mom to carry a bundle of gear the size of a Volkswagen with a 35-pound kid tucked amongst it. "I'm just kind of used to it," I protested, but the consensus of incredulity began to undermine my confidence.

I was pretty sure my kids were safe from rabid wolves and August frostbite, but that didn't stop me from worrying. What if we ran out of M&M's? What if we fainted from the fumes of four pairs of wet socks in a three-person tent? What if Lizzy woke everyone in camp at 3:30 a.m. when plush friend Lamby became temporarily lost in the abyss of her sleeping bag? What if (oh, the horror) Jay and I— along with Jay's dad and forty-five total strangers—were subjected to thirty-three miles of twins-in-stereo whining?

In the week before the hike, as I packed up six zillion miniature Ziplocs of honey roasted peanuts, dried cranberries, and Tootsie Pops, I tried to talk myself out of my peer-induced paranoia. The kids were experienced hikers. They liked Powerbars. They had warm—albeit mismatched—homemade long johns and rain gear, and I could still get away with dressing them that way, since they hadn't yet realized Mommy wasn't cool. Earlier in the summer, they had demonstrated that they could be entertained for four hours at a time, hiking through impenetrable fog, by my attempts to narrate all of "James and the Giant Peach" and the "Wizard of Oz". Given that most adults would start hyperventilating after thirty seconds of my rendition of "Yellow Brick Road," I felt like we'd done pretty well. But still, I was apprehensive.

Short legs takes small steps, but they nonetheless climbed the infamous Golden Stairs over the Chilkoot pass. FAMILY PHOTO

The preschoolers were shocked and fascinated to learn that the Klondike gold miners were litterbugs.
FAMILY PHOTO

Once we hit the trail, the questions grew even more urgent, and I proffered my rehearsed rationale for bringing the kids on a hike that the guidebooks and websites describe as "rugged" and "very challenging." Their daddy grew up here, I explained. Well, not here, in this lean-to, but in the small town of Skagway, where we all started. Their grandpa—now sixty-eight years old, and striding along the trail far ahead of us—served as the ranger for this National Park for more than a decade. This wasn't just a fun jaunt, it was more of a family pilgrimage.

Of course, the whole explanation was disingenuous, coming from me. I'd never been to the Chilkoot before—though it was a fun jaunt. But everyone seemed at least partially placated.

The most immediate downside was their inevitable rush toward my father-in-law with questions about the park. There are no backwoods vacations for people wearing Park Service green pants.

The real Park Service employees were as dubious as everyone else. "The day over the pass takes the average hiker ten hours," one of them pronounced, looking at us meaningfully. Cowed, we departed from camp at 7 a.m. that morning, expecting everyone else to overtake us along the way. As it turned out, little kids are

> **TIP ▪ Fun with Preschoolers**
>
> Jay recalls that during this stage we engaged in many, many different games to keep the twins from getting bored:
>
> "Songs were sung, words were spelled, riddles were told, snacks were eaten. One of the more popular games involved a ferocious dragon who asked the twins questions, like for example how to spell 'dog' or what was 12 plus 5. If the twins got the answer correct the dragon would roar and gnash its teeth. This was so popular that soon the twins reversed things and had the dragon asking ME questions, like 'what is 1000 plus 1000', and my favorite, 'How many lakes are there in Alaska?' Tricky dragon!"

substantially more squirrel-like than are middle-aged cubicle-dwellers. Hours went by, and no one passed us. Rocks were fun. Despite the fog, there was plenty to see along the way: big, rusty, exciting stuff.

"The long-ago gold miners were litterbugs," announced Lizzy, with all the righteous indignation of a kid who has learned and internalized the rules. If children are chastised for dropping paper scraps or fruit stickers, then how did those gold-rushers get away with leaving hundreds of cans, the soles of countless pairs of worn-out shoes, and mysterious yet fascinating pulleys, winches, levers, and gears? Ah, but this was not trash, I told her—these were artifacts. Artifacts! It sounded important. "Look, another artifact!" she informed me, every three feet. Up, up, we went.

At the summit, the ranger on duty appeared from a tiny cabin that seemed to be perched on the edge of nothing, wind-swept and wild. News of our group had preceded us by radio. He peered at the kids as if expecting to see open sores, blood, or signs of extreme emotional distress. Perhaps he was hoping for the chance to make a Child Social Services report from the mountains of British Colombia. "We don't usually see 'em below eight," he grunted. Molly and Lizzy told him about artifacts, around mouthfuls of peanut butter and jelly.

We'd made it safely to the far side of the dastardly pass, and the twins had just started a busy game of Making Pretend Stuff with Twigs and Moss in the Drizzle. Our fellow hikers' meals progressed from chili mac to cherry cobbler to chunks of chocolate. Latecomers, looking as if they'd spent the day with the Spanish Inquisitors, staggered into camp.

"Do you remember?" asked Molly. She has a penchant for talking about events from a few hours or days previously as if they happened eons ago. "Do you remember, there was a stove at the top?"

This, I had to admit, had impressed me too, because I always like finding evidence that someone else is a bigger idiot than I am. The Klondike would-be-gold-miners had hiked endlessly in the dead

After summiting the pass on the Alaska side of the Chilkoot Trail, the four-year-olds ambled into Canada.
FAMILY PHOTO

> The only part I remember of the rainbow is standing on a big rock and trying to button up Mom's shirt–to turn around and find the rainbow gone. Talk about tragedy!
> –Lizzy, remembering the ephemeral

of the Subarctic winter, ferrying four hundred pounds of flour, one hundred fifty pounds of bacon, and dense-sounding items such as scythe stones, whipsaws, and oakum. They hauled stoves to the top of mountains, and abandoned them. Those who didn't haul their goods themselves fronted money to pay others—often local Tlingit people—to do it for them. Stampeders were counting on finding gold. Almost without exception, they did not.

A scenic summer stroll with a couple of kids seemed positively sensible in comparison. None of us were carrying oakum or looking for gold, which is perhaps why the hike seemed so much easier to me than I'd expected. We'd been getting to camp each day by midafternoon. There was plenty of time left to play Make A Hat For Mommy Out of Lichen, and to pick blueberries.

A few of the less travel-worn folks wandered over to chat. More than one hiker mentioned it was a little demoralizing to struggle along the trail all day, only to be greeted by kids too short to go eyeball-to-hip-belt with you. But the dubiousness and disapproval I'd sensed two days ago seemed to be evaporating. Our new-found friends commended the kids on their hiking prowess, and took photos of them. They asked Molly and Lizzy what they liked best about the trail. They offered more chocolate. After twenty miles, a national boundary, and several long hours of precipitous scrambling on the misty pass, it seemed the twins had earned their stripes, blinking train-logo sneakers and all. By association, Jay, his dad, and I had gained the provisional status of Maybe Not Insane Guardians.

Three generations completed the 33-mile Chilkoot Trail together. FAMILY PHOTO

Montana Guy was taking a trip down memory lane. "This is such a great age . . . I remember when my kids were that small . . . it seems like just yesterday . . ." His eighteen-year old daughter, to her credit, was keeping her eye-rolling to a minimum.

The rain was ending, and a lean grey-haired man, more energized than the rest, walked a hundred feet up the nearest hummock of rock to check out the view. A few moments later he called down to the rest of us, "A rainbow! Come on up and see!"

A rainbow—the stuff of a thousand wobbly-crayoned art projects! The kids were up the hill in a flash, leaping and shrieking their joy. A rainbow! With all the colors! A moment later it dipped into a full arc. Then it doubled.

A few others joined us on the hilltop, but the rest stayed below, either too weary or too jaded to bother. Those of us in the rainbow clique shook our heads at their lack of initiative.

Five minutes after it appeared, the rainbow faded. The kids' joy, however, did not. They scampered from rock to rock, effervescent on excitement and chocolate. "Do you remember?" said Molly. "It had purple and red and orange! Do you remember? It was double!"

Montana Guy smiled at me. "Those are the happiest kids I've ever seen," he remarked.

Well, they certainly weren't the cleanest, or the most polite, and they probably weren't the smartest or most coordinated either. But after all my jitters, I realized I could never have asked for a better compliment.

But How Do You Deal with . . . Wildlife

Friends and family from outside Alaska often seem fixated on the dangers of our local wildlife, particularly bears. In my experience, many people over-exaggerate the dangers of bears, but underestimate the dangers of moose. For the most part, fears are overblown. But especially with young children in tow, knowing your wildlife—and teaching the same to your kids—is common sense.

Moose

In the parking lot of the Denali National Park Visitor's Center, during a recent visit, a young moose cow was calmly browsing on willow. Gaggles of tourists were taking her photo, which was cool. They were also getting way too close—which wasn't cool at all.

Sure, moose are vegetarians. But they're really big—up to fifteen hundred pounds big. And they can kick. Or charge. Males can be unpredictable and territorial, and females will go to any length to protect their young.

Spotting backyard moose is one of the benefits of living in Alaska—so long as they're spotted from a safe distance. FAMILY PHOTO

Luckily, it's fairly easy to avoid being tromped or impaled. Make your presence known, give them a wide berth, and for heaven's sake, don't try for a photo op six feet from those hooves.

The single greatest danger with regard to moose, though, has nothing to do with their hooves and everything to do with their stupidity around roads. They like to browse on the young vegetation that grows up at roadsides. They are tall enough that, when struck, they can come straight through your windshield, bringing their three quarters of a ton in weight with them.

Long story short, don't mess with moose. And if you're in an area with elk or muskoxen or bison, ditto with them too. Just don't.

So yes, I sent a ranger out to manage the crowds at the Visitor Center. I guess I can be a killjoy.

Bears

Lest my introduction sound dismissive, I'll admit that yes, bears can be dangerous. The threat they pose should not be taken lightly. But in all our years of enjoying the great outdoors in Alaska, we've never had a dangerous bear encounter. We've seen bears—at a distance, on many hikes, or relatively close, on the Denali Park Road. We've seen tons of bear prints, bear-scratched trees, and juicy-berry bear poop. But the bears have left us alone. Sometimes we carry bear spray, but when we're in less risky territory, we don't even do that.

Bear spray and other weaponry are poor substitutes for bear-safe behavior. Bear-safe behavior requires understanding how bears think, and anticipating what could go wrong.

Never, ever get close to bears, startle them, or get between mama and her cubs. Never walk through dense brush without making continuous noise. Sing! Tell knock-knock jokes!

Be incredibly careful about food, and teach your kids to be careful, too. This may include a high level of vigilance with regard to normal kid levels of crumbs, spills, and smears. Never tempt bears with food or waste not properly stored in a cabin, vehicle, bear canister, or properly designed bear-hang. Read up on how to keep a clean camp and store food properly; there are a lot of resources on this.

Also read about the differences between black bears, grizzlies (brown bears), and polar bears. Learn how to react if faced by each species. And then avoid polar bears at all costs. They're the ones who may actually be looking for you as dinner.

If you do carry spray, make sure you understand how to use it, can deploy it quickly at any moment, but have no chance of triggering it by mistake.

Of course, one advantage of winter adventures is that the bears are snoozing. Sleep tight, bears.

Porcupines

Porkies are slow, waddling, innocent creatures, and of no danger to most humans, but they deserve a brief mention because many dog owners live in fear of porcupine encounters. We've had a few with our dogs. Such run-ins instantly turn a delightful stroll or hike into a miserable disaster—and not just for the canine. Trying to get quills out of a dog in the backcountry is no joke. Bring pliers, such as those included in a Leatherman tool. In most cases, a vet is required to get them all—and a vet might be a long, long way away.

If you are already contending with the needs of young kids on your trip, a dog/porcupine encounter could leave you in a particularly difficult position. The best defense is good dog training, vigilance, and—although being able to run free is a great joy to dogs in remote areas—use of a leash as needed.

I have never heard of a curious young child getting quilled, but the mere thought is terrible. If your toddler is old enough to run, be sure to emphasize just how scary and un-pettable the prickly creatures are. And if your child is too young to listen to reason . . . well, kid-leashes are available too.

Everything Else

"Everything else" covers a lot, I know. Here in interior Alaska, it includes a wide range of birds (redpolls, gray jays, ravens, chickadees, and various raptors and owls, just to name a few) plus a wealth of small mammals (voles, shrews, squirrels, hares, marmots, and more).

It also covers elusive predators such as wolves, coyotes, and lynxes. We have caribou. We have plenty of insects (some might say too many, but that's covered elsewhere) and our token frog, the wood frog. We're entirely lacking in snakes. Zero snakes.

Needless to say, all these creatures are entirely different from one another. They're fascinating to learn about and to watch, and can be a huge plus in luring kids into the great outdoors. Bugs! Furry things! Tracks! Poop! Antlers! I heartily encourage learning about the local fauna (and flora), and passing this info on. But as far as hazards go, there are really only a small number of things to say about "everything else": don't feed it; don't leave your food out where it can help itself; don't try to tame it; don't try to catch or kill it unless you have the right sort of hunting or fishing license and you know what you're doing; don't let your dog chase it, and if any critter is behaving oddly, give it an extra wide birth.

Kids can quickly learn to both love and respect wildlife. And they'll love all the singing and knock-knock jokes too.

This photo was taken from the window of a Denali Park bus; while on bikes, we maintained a much greater distance. FAMILY PHOTO

Adventure is in the Mind of the Adventurer

"This week, instead of writing down the titles of the books you've read, we want you to tell us about adventures you've had." The librarian in the Berry Room was smiling at Molly and Lizzy. I looked at them expectantly, too. Adventure! The connotations were irresistible. I knew I loved adventure.

Molly was half-clinging to my leg, but she was enticed by both the appeal of the question and the charisma of the questioner. She ventured an answer: "There was a big big storm and we had to hide under the picnic table roof thing."

Wait, what? I thought. The thunderstorm last weekend at the Manley Hot Springs campground was not in any way a real adventure!

Granite Tors Trail Loop

Location ▪ Chena River Recreation Area, east of Fairbanks.

Distance and duration ▪ 15 miles, one overnight (though a day hike with older kids at age 12).

Locomotion ▪ Hiking, with kids walking most of the time, and at other times riding in Sherpani kid-carrier packs loaded with all our gear.

Terrain ▪ Hilly, but with a clear and well-marked trail.

Weather ▪ Very hot and sunny, over 80°F.

Accommodations ▪ Small trail shelter for emergency use only. Tent camping. Limited water availability, and water must be treated.

However, the librarian gave every indication of genuine interest. Her enthusiasm encouraged my shy children to wax loquacious, non-linearly of course.

"We ran a real race," Lizzy offered. "The big kids winned." Lizzy didn't like being beaten. "But," she added in self-consolation, "they were almost teenagers."

Adventure. I ruminated. A few years previously, pre-kids, I'd debated the nuances of this single word with Jay and my friends Tom and Justin for an entire hike's length around the Granite Tors Trail. The route is a fifteen-mile loop with steep ascents, dramatic vistas, impressive rock formations, and sucking bogs, so we had plenty of time to talk. For me it felt like the perfect locale to discuss the subject of adventure.

The nice book lady wanted to listen while Mommy was distracted by her own thoughts, and Molly and Lizzy had lots more to relate. "Daddy's bike had two flat tires, but we didn't mind because we played with the tickle grass."

The Tors trail and I already had a bit of history. Jay lured me to the Tors as our first real date, telling me he knew a "nice afternoon hike." On that occasion, the loop took us from noon to 6 p.m., so he maintains that his description was precisely accurate. I didn't argue the point at the time, because I like long hikes, and I didn't want to look like a wimp in front of this sweet blue-eyed boy I'd recently met. As I sweated and squelched my way over rocks, tussocks, and logs, trying not to suck air as I chatted with my date, I savored the feeling of adventure.

I tuned the kids in and out: "We went to Seattle. Steve and Manish have a dog called Billy." Um, okay. A miniature dachshund is an adventure?

Several years later, strolling along with Jay, Tom, and Justin, with a well-practiced knowledge of the trail and nothing to prove, the hike didn't feel particularly adventuresome to me. Justin had disagreed.

Kids to librarian: "On the way down the mountain, we were a mushing team, but only walking, because Anna didn't want to run."

True adventure, Jay and Tom had argued, requires novelty. It implies a visceral thrill, a flutter of excitement, and a sense of risk.

"I liked Ireland. There were snails." This was a remarkably patient librarian. She seemed genuinely interested in adventure-snails.

In the debate between Jay and Tom and Justin, I wavered. I knew the Tors could be an adventure. I felt peeved when Tom and Jay mocked meager exploits, but I wasn't sure what was making me so defensive. I never entirely took Justin's side in the argument, either.

"We have our own sled. Togiak and Polar are old, but Remus is bouncy."

If the Tors were novel and thrilling on my first visit because I'd found a date who shared my proclivity for muddy hiking boots, they were novel and thrilling on my second trip there for slightly different reasons. In October of 1999, several months into our relationship, Jay and I hiked the trail again. We were hit by an unexpected white-out, with snow heavy enough to obscure our tracks within minutes of making them. We tried to short-cut off the ridge by hugging the side of the hill slope, but we failed. In the darkness of an early-winter afternoon, we peered at our compass and soggy map and realized we had dropped into the wrong valley.

We were a daunting distance from the car. We weren't lost, precisely, but the slog out through the rapidly piling white stuff was long. Very long. By the time we staggered back to the parking lot, dug out the vehicle, and inched our way back to town on snow-clogged roads, it was 5 a.m. We scarfed down spaghetti for breakfast. Despite my exhaustion and my shame at having made such a silly wrong turn, I was buoyed by the feeling of adventure.

> We used to think the boat loop (a six-mile loop of trail by our house) was super-long. But now that we're thirteen, we can snow-bike the whole thing in less than an hour.
> –Molly, on how relative distance changes with age

"Daddy and I raced the butterflies. One of them beated us."

After that hike with Tom and Justin, Jay and I didn't hike the Tors for four years. During that time, our universe shifted. When we hit the trail again in 2009, it took us not one afternoon, but two days to complete the fifteen miles. For about five of those miles, our two three-year-olds hopped and meandered around our feet. For the other ten miles, our packs were heavy. It was our first attempt at real backpacking with the kids. We were trying out our ultra-light gear, which under the circumstances didn't feel all that light. We had to be prepared to protect our precious progeny against voracious mosquitoes, hot sun, and wind-driven 40-degree rain. We had to bring bedtime stories, stuffed animals, sippy cups, and footie pajamas. We were trusting the kids not to whine, not to rebel, and not to wet their pants. We were seeing the trail through their eyes, as they exclaimed over tree fungus and stopped to worship puddles, ladybugs, and cloudberries. For them, life was full of challenge, risk, and excitement.

"The boat loop is five miles!"

Standing in the public library's Berry Room, listening with embarrassment and amusement to a breathless recitation of mundane events, I finally realized why I was so ungenerous in my willingness to grant the title of "adventure" to the kids' latest bike ride, or a bus trip taken by tourists, or Justin's ascent of the Tors. It wasn't that I couldn't accept that these experiences should be judged subjectively. It's simply that I was worried, and perversely jealous. I'd already seen lots of thunderstorms. I loved adventure—I thrived on adventure—and I was secretly afraid that a lot of my adventures had already been trumped by experience, and therefore "used up."

"We're digging a big hole, for treasure, or maybe dinosaur bones."

Of course, my worries were ridiculous. Identifying my own hang-up was a relief, because as soon as the thought formed, I could logically and laughingly quash it. Who did I think I was, anyhow? Sacagawea? Sir Francis Drake? I hadn't even used up all the easy-to-reach adventures, let alone the ones that required a bit more planning, expensive plane tickets, and new outfits.

I hadn't bicycled to the Arctic Ocean and taken a bracing dip amidst the sea ice. I hadn't gone sea kayaking in Prince William Sound. I hadn't ridden in a hot air balloon. I hadn't even seen the Grand Canyon, for heaven's sake. The world was a large and fabulously complex place, with billions of inhabitants, thousands of ecosystems, and entire continents I had yet to visit. I could no more use up all the possible adventures than I could suddenly speak Yoruba. Hadn't I been paying attention to the theme of the summer reading program? One World—Many Stories. Or many adventures, as the case may be.

"We biked all the way to Pioneer Park."

Mollified and cheered, I tried to rescue the Berry Room librarian. I smiled at her apologetically as I redirected Molly and Lizzy toward the picture books. "We go biking and hiking kind of a lot," I said, in an attempt to excuse all the unnecessary detail still being over-shared.

"Mommy and Daddy don't have to carry us anymore. Not like when we were little."

The librarian still seemed interested. She told me she'd been doing a bit of hiking recently, too. Where were we planning on going this summer?

"We get to have juice when we go hiking. And pudding every day!"

"Well, we want to see how far the kids can manage completely under their own steam this year," I said. "We were thinking of doing Pinnell, and maybe Kesugi, but we'll probably start with the Tors."

The librarian looked surprised, but she was all smiles. "Wow . . . well, good luck! I hiked the Granite Tors last weekend. It's a beautiful trail, but I'm still sore." She laughed. "It was a real adventure."

She was right, of course. I knew that then. There were and are, after all, an unbounded number and flavor of adventures still beckoning.

To young children, seeing a giant snail (top) can be as much of an "adventure" as camping at a remote site on the Granite Tors ridge (bottom). FAMILY PHOTOS

Time for Yourself: Being Epic

The winter when the twins were three, Jay competed in the inaugural annual White Mountains 100—backcountry skiing a hundred miles through wild Alaskan forests and mountains, slogging up long ascents, struggling over a windy four thousand-foot mountain pass, and barreling down what the event officially describes as "bowel-clenching descents." Temperatures dropped to twenty below zero. Ice, slush, bumps, tussocks, and ruts abounded. It took him over thirty sleepless hours.

While Jay skied, I stayed home playing mom. The kids and I made congratulatory welcome-home signs, did some baking, and organized the post-race party, at which the racers all said overly kind things about the cheap Sam's Club spaghetti, the veggies and dip, and the cake decorated by preschool artisans. I felt tubby and torpid in a roomful of people with less body fat than Olympic gymnasts. I saw the frostbite-blistered fingers, toes, and noses, and I listened to the epic stories.

The White Mountains 100

Location ▪ The BLM White Mountains Recreation Area, north of Fairbanks.

Distance and duration ▪ 100 miles, as long as it takes (in this case, 35 hours; I have since done it much faster on a fat-tired snow bike).

Locomotion ▪ Cross-country skis, with minimal gear in a day pack.

Terrain ▪ Variable, with a high pass above tree line. Mostly wide and well-packed trail, but areas of ice, overflow (water on top of ice), and soft snow.

Weather ▪ Sunny and pleasant late winter conditions, above freezing by day and about 10°F at night (but highly variable for this event, year to year, with temperatures sometimes dropping to -20°F).

Accommodations ▪ Water, snacks, and a heated shelter at checkpoints (cabins) about every 20 miles. Two medics on snowmachines out on the course. A heated trailer at the start/finish.

Certain members of my social circle like to use the word "epic" in its adjectival form to describe adventures that incorporate all the best components of, say, Homer's Odyssey. Are there seemingly impossible quests involved? Pain and suffering? Blood-thirsty many-headed sea creatures? Epic. On the other hand, outdoor adventures that include designated campgrounds, bedtime stories, or marshmallow roasts may be fun, but they aren't epic.

Several of my friends had completed the race, and they were happy to share the details of their odysseys. Tom admitted that near the finish, snow-bent boreal spruce trees started to look like people. He began peering over his shoulder in sleep-deprived paranoia. His knees were swollen from repeatedly crashing on sheer sloping ice. Amy, who received the perseverance award after thirty-eight grueling hours, told me about high-velocity impacts between her face and the snow. She said she spent hours longing to glimpse the next little white sign promising "one mile to checkpoint." She was terribly dehydrated, yet unable to eat or drink. Meanwhile Jay, in characteristically self-effacing fashion, said that his biggest concern was the poor job he did cleaning up the trail after he sullied it with partially digested ramen and coffee.

Jay then went on to protest that the race was "fun." Lots of fun, he insisted. Boy, was he excited to do it again, he told me. When the time to register for the 2011 race rolled around, he stayed up until midnight to make sure he garnered a slot.

So did I.

Don't get me wrong, I'm not a masochist. At least, I don't think I'm a masochist. I signed up for the race because I love backcountry skiing and because I wanted to challenge myself—not because I actively desired pain, misery, suppurating blisters, or delirium.

Still, there were issues of pride at stake. In recent years, Jay had done a lot of trips that made for really excellent stories. I—in part because of our two fabulous little fans of campgrounds, bedtime stories, and marshmallows—had fewer tales to tell. As much as I wanted to experience the race, and notwithstanding my preference to avoid frostbite, hypothermia, and regurgitation, at some level I wanted my Odysseus story, in all its drama-queen glory. I wanted to be epic.

Thanks to a truly magnificent set of friends who were willing to babysit twin preschoolers, Jay and I were both able to register for the 2011 event. But by the time late March rolled around, I was more than a little worried. Who did I think I was, anyhow? Not an ultra-racer, certainly. Besides, I knew I hadn't trained enough. No, that was too generous. I hadn't really trained at all. My total skiing for the winter added up to about three hundred miles, which is far too little for someone who plans to cover a third of that distance in one event, mostly nonstop.

The remainder of my physical exertion had consisted of commuting four miles to my job at the university, by bike or on foot, towing or pushing the kids in their nifty convertible Chariot trailer. Granted, jogging eight miles round trip with two four-year-olds can work up a sweat, but it doesn't exactly qualify one to cover the length of four marathons in a row.

At the pre-race meeting, I was reminded of the fact that most of the people I'd met at the previous year's party had visible sinews, complex competitive strategies, and dozens of ultra-races under their belts. A BLM ranger sat mute at the back of the room for a full hour before offering, as a parting one-liner, the information that an early-waking bear had been sighted near Borealis. "Early bears are hungry," he noted, as if a roomful of Alaskans might think it was a good idea to smear themselves with peanut butter and honey. I won a coveted door prize at the meeting, but worried that if I didn't make it through the race, I'd feel guilty about keeping it.

When I dug in my ski poles at the start, I was sure that at some point in the next two days I was going to begin hating snow . . . and hating trees . . . and hating my skis, my backpack, all the free audio books I'd downloaded from the library, and every Ziploc of Cadbury's Dark, Nutter Butters, Combos, and peanut-butter-and-jelly-on-pilot-bread that I had packed for myself. In fact, I was pretty sure that somewhere along the hundred-mile course I was going to assume a personality that blended the least likeable attributes of Eeyore, Marvin the depressed android, and a partially decayed zombie. I wasn't sure that I should be out there at all—but in the face of all that, I was expecting the race to at least be epic.

I hung back, watching the speedsters disappear up the first hill in a jostling rush. The early part of the trail was backyard-familiar to me, all rolling landscapes and easily-earned views across valleys of dark spruce and sun-reflecting snow. The early morning sky warmed to a deepening blue. I shared a few upbeat words with my fellow slowpokes, and at mile seven I smiled for my friend Ned's camera, but by mile ten I was skiing alone, in a private sunlit world of shushing snow. I was stripped down to a tank top.

Conditions in late March can range from icy slush that forces you to coat your skis in hideously gummy klister, to the -25°F temps and howling wind that had almost frozen Amy's feet at the top of the pass the previous year. This year, the sun warmed the snow just enough to make it slick and quick, but not enough to wreck it. I was slathered in sunscreen, mock-hip in cheap sunglasses, and basking in Vitamin D. After a long Subarctic winter, spring feels like a revelation. Constant entertainment streamed in through my headphones— novels carefully selected to include nothing in the emotional range of Steven King or Jack London. I had forgotten just how starkly beautiful the blackened stems of an old wildfire burn can be, or how friendly broad tree trunks can look in the valley bottoms. I had

The top of Cache Mountain pass in Alaska's White Mountains is fifty miles from the Elliott Highway trailhead in either direction. FAMILY PHOTO

forgotten how much I like having someone read stories aloud to me.

At mile seventeen, the first checkpoint was a flurry of goodwill and free cocoa refills. At mile twenty-six, affable strangers called hellos over the ecstatic barking of their dog team; apparently watching sixty-five people race past was canine nirvana. I managed the precipitous drop to Beaver Creek without removing my skis or shattering anything, and I made it to the second checkpoint at mile thirty-nine feeling optimistic enough to grin for the race volunteer wielding a camera. The long ascent to the Cache Mountain Divide lay ahead, but I had a foil-wrapped, cheese-filled baked potato in one hand, and the sun was still shining.

The next eight hours were slow and dreamlike. The trail wove through mile upon mile of grey-green forest, rolling over hillocks, but tending ever upward. The sky darkened, and snow began to fall. At last, the trees thinned around me until I was surrounded by sheer white, windblown and austere. I reached the top of the pass just as the very last glimmer of daylight disappeared. The tracks of all those who had crossed ahead of me were already being subsumed by fresh snow and wind. Visibility by headlamp narrows to a half-dozen feet in a swirl of snowflakes, a phenomenon that I partly blame for my snaillike progress—even when gravity again began to work in my favor. Flying headlong down the slopes seemed ill-advised. I picked my way across the sloping surface of the notorious ice lakes with my feet slush-protected by plastic bags that had once contained wood pellets, and anti-skidded with Yak Trax. It was no doubt a stylish getup. The medics' wall tent glowed temptingly, but I replied to a cheery greeting by explaining that I was doing just fine, thanks. I waddled on by.

Any dramatic claims I might have made about mind-altering fatigue or about pulling an all-nighter alone in the dark were negated by the three-hour nap I took at Windy Gap checkpoint, at mile sixty-two. After consuming at least half a box of crackers, I lay down fully clothed on a wooden bench amidst a cacophony of comings and goings. Three fellow racers were exchanging past stories around the rough wooden table. Someone had been frozen into her own snowshoe bindings on some three hundred-mile trek. It sounded epic. I snored.

When I hit the trail again at 5 a.m., it was still dark—but I felt rejuvenated, even ebullient. Who wouldn't, gliding through a winter wonderland of new-falling snow, listening to Bill Bryson's sweetly mid-Atlantic voice reading aloud the comic escapades of his 1950s childhood, munching through four chocolate chip cookies?

It was soon after this Breakfast of Champions that I experienced what could have qualified as drama. I practically ran over the obstacle before I saw it. It was a person, lying in the snow beside the trail. Face down.

I had about two seconds for all my first-aid training to run through my head in completely random order before I realized that the guy I was now stooping over was neither hypothermic nor the tragic victim of marauding Yetis, but merely asleep. I had two more seconds of confused indecision before he woke up, sprang to his feet, and showered me with thanks and apology. He'd told himself he'd lie down for just one song, he explained, pointing sheepishly to his headphones.

The fresh snow made for particularly slow progress. The sun rose as I passed the dramatic limestone jags near Caribou Bluff. They towered over me on both sides, simultaneously protective and intimidating. The mottled light filtering through dense clouds was as gorgeous as the nighttime snowfall and the clear hot skies of the previous day had been.

Throughout that slow second morning, the weather was all magic and no skullduggery. The temperature did not plummet. The icy sections of trail were at a minimum, and I did not plunge any limbs into liquid slush. No starving bears appeared. The views from the previous day were veiled, but not obscured. Mile upon mile, valley upon valley, in every direction, lay forests, marshlands, rivers, crags. No roads. No houses. No overpasses, no strip malls, no car alarms, no Walmarts. I was soaking in the tranquility.

At mile eighty-two, the volunteer at the Borealis checkpoint snapped another photo. In it, I am holding a bowl of ramen noodles and crushed Fritos, and wearing an expression that implies I am delightedly anticipating the next crunchy-soggy, tepid, salt-infused spoonful. At mile ninety-one, further photo evidence was recorded: I'm beaming like a kid at her own birthday party—albeit a sweaty and perhaps slightly deranged one.

By the last ten miles of the race, all familiar territory, I was undeniably stiff and sore. I'd suffered from weak Achilles tendons for years, and they were starting to remind me of their displeasure. Crouching down for potty breaks seemed a lot more challenging than it had the previous day, and I began to regret my hot cocoa consumption. When I reached the unrelenting mile of hill known as "Wickersham Wall" it seemed expedient not only to remove my skis, but also to walk backward all the way up it. Three miles later, at the bottom of the last steep downhill, the effort of rigorous snowplowing ski technique made me think that my knees and ankles might enjoy a one-minute rest, which is why I was lying ignominiously in the trail when not one but three dog sleds came barreling down at me. Alas, climbing a small mountain in reverse and flailing stiff-legged in front of thirty confused canines doesn't count to me as epic— especially not if one is also listening to Dave Barry's Greatest Hits, and giggling.

I completed the race—without grievous bodily harm, dalliances with bears, or even a single blister—in exactly thirty-five hours, placing me fifty-fourth out of sixty-five entrants. Since seven people didn't finish, there were actually only four behind me. Three of them were walking the course. I was pokey—though not quite slow enough for the perseverance award. I never got dehydrated or cold. I never needed the medics' extensive first aid kits, or even my own, which had consisted exclusively of pain killers and duct tape. I was pleased to have an excuse to consume enough cheese sandwiches and Reisen chocolates to fuel an army. In my mind, my pace, my health, and my diet were decidedly non-epic.

At the end of the race, a stalwart volunteer snapped one final photo. I am holding one of my kids in each arm, and grinning at Jay. Clearly, if I was still strong enough to lift seventy-five pounds of preschooler, I couldn't have been working hard enough. The four of us don't look epic—we look like Family Circle.

I hosted the post-race party again. It felt different from the previous year—but not exactly in the way I'd expected. My co-organizer contributed some fresh bread and heaps of strawberries, melon, and pineapple, to the menu, and everyone was even kinder in their thanks. I still felt dumpy compared to most of the crowd, but I cared less. That first year, I was looking forward to the 2012 race because I was jealous of all the epic-ness around me. In 2012, I realized to my own surprise, I was looking forward to the next year's race for a whole different list of reasons.

Wilderness inspires me. Exercise invigorates me. I now had an official time to beat, and I do love a challenge. But most importantly, it dawned on me that in my life as a busy working mom, there are only rare respites in which I can experience the bliss of being on a mountaintop at sunset, or having hour after hour all to myself, or absorbing an entire novel nonstop, or eating a gigantic Cadbury bar without even a twinge of remorse. To do all these things at once? Epic.

Ages 5–6: We Can Do It!

No More Being Carried

Lots of new things occur when kids are five and six. The tooth fairy. The school bus. Numbers that go beyond the normal complement of fingers and toes. And—in our family, at least—this age heralded real locomotive autonomy.

Not that I haven't given Molly and Lizzy piggy-back rides since then; I'm a stalwart fan of piggy-back rides. But on the trail, once they turned five, the kids hiked on their own. And on two wheels, the additional wheels of the bike trailer were traded in for one-wheeled tag-along (trail-behind) bikes of both the double and single variety.

We were playing it by ear, of course. Results may vary. But at five, Molly and Lizzy gamely walked ten miles, and pedaled on tag-alongs—wait, how far did they go? Fifty miles? You'd think I'd remember, but maybe the fact that I don't is a good indicator that is was (mostly) no big deal.

Of course, "mostly" covers a lot of ground. Legs were still short, and so were attention spans. The pace was slow. And plenty of motivation was needed, in the form of games, songs, stories, study of landmarks, identification of wildlife poop, carving names on the underside of fungus, and consumption of wildly unhealthy treats.

As a family we're generally pretty healthy eaters, when we're at home. But you might not believe that if you saw our trail snacks. In addition to more reasonable items such as pilot bread with peanut butter, trail mix, and granola bars, we're connoisseurs of the candy and chip brands of multiple continents.

In part, this started as positive reinforcement: the kids quickly learned that they only got junk food while exerting themselves. But it was practical, too. While children have lots of energy, they burn through fuel quickly. While hiking, skiing, or biking, they need to eat more frequently than you'd readily believe. The slow sugar-infusion of a lollipop prevents a surge and crash, and can keep a four-year-old trucking over the Chilkoot Pass. Plus—yay, lollipop!

If the treats are themselves a source of entertainment, even better. We were not above buying things with a prize inside, or things shaped like other things, or cookies made to look (vaguely) like animals or letters. Gummy things of all varieties have featured heavily over the years. I think candy necklaces have happened at some point.

In cold weather, hot chocolate is a crucial food group. Bringing a thermos on the trail adds weight, but can be a huge morale-booster.

An additional tip, important with this age group, is to avoid

At five years old, the kids proudly hiked on their own—here exploring the site of a recent forest fire on Tabletop Mountain. FAMILY PHOTO

weighing the kids down. Small kids want to carry packs, because packs look cool. Obviously. But small kids are already slow— sometimes agonizingly so—and even the slightest of burdens makes them slower. For as long as possible, we persuaded our kids not to carry anything. At about age six, they were granted the right to carry tiny day-packs, containing just their own snacks and perhaps their rain gear. They didn't get "real" full packs until age nine.

Even then, a hefty twenty-five-percent-of-bodyweight load for a fifty-pound person is . . . well, you do the math. And as of age thirteen, some of our kids' peers have reached almost adult size, but Molly and Lizzy are still small. Today, they're now full-speed and full-enthusiasm participants in our adventures, but they aren't yet full beasts of burden. And they also still enjoy the calorie-burst and morale-boost of some trail snacks of questionable nutritional merit.

The Grownups Get the Broken Cookies: Lessons in Empathy

"But I want a WHOLE cookie!"

Lizzy's woebegone plea seemed to voice the opinions of all three five-year-olds. They trio of them were staring in conster-nation at the package of Rasp-berry Chocolate Milanos, unable to fathom how the bag might have become just a tad squashed in Jay's backpack during the ten-mile journey to Tolovana Hot Springs—over mountains, ice, and imaginary-troll-infested swamps.

"Don't worry," I said, "The grownups get the broken ones."

My friend Ned, father of Anna, the child who sometimes made my twins look like triplets—smiled wryly. "Sounds like the title of a book," he remarked.

He had a point. I'd made my crumb-eating promise entirely without thinking about it, but now my words rattled around in my tired brain like the delicate cookies in the bag I was holding. What I'd said was true enough—I did always get the broken ones. In the same vein, I gave the kids the coveted seats, the softer towels, and

Tolovana Hot Springs

Location ▪ Private leased property, 2.5 hour drive northwest of Fairbanks.

Distance and duration ▪ 20 miles round trip, with two days of hiking and a rest day (two overnights at the hot springs).

Locomotion ▪ Hiking, with kids hiking the full distance and adults carrying all the gear.

Terrain ▪ Hilly, with a clear and well-marked trail, but 2-3 miles of swampy lowlands.

Weather ▪ Clear and sunny fall weather, around 50°F.

Accommodations ▪ Comfortable rental cabins with bunks, wood stoves, propane stoves, and solar/LED lighting. Rustic natural hot tubs.

Chatting with a friend is an excellent way to enjoy the ten mile hike to remote Tolovana Hot Springs.
FAMILY PHOTO

the warmer blankets. I'd eat the peach that required complex anti-fungal vivisection, while offering my children the ones that look like they came from the Sunnydale Farm of Genetically Engineered Fruit-Spheres. Whenever vagaries in quality occurred, I routinely took whatever was rustier, damper, squishier, browner, or squeakier. And yet I'd never really questioned why—or whether it was a good idea.

Was I merely trying to avoid the whining that accompanies childish disappointments? If so, broken-cookie-consumption qualifies as a form of . . . spoiling! Horrors! Whenever I saw parents in Fred Meyers caving to high-pitched nagging for Choco-Breakfast-Yumyums or Super Plastic Action Crap-ola, I felt smug about my own no-rewards-for-whining policies. But maybe I needed to eat a heaping serving of my own self-righteousness along with those pulverized Milanos.

TIP ▪ Trail Games, Kindergarten Level

Jay recalls from our Tolovana trip that "The ice-covered puddles gave the little people loads of entertainment. Molly even found a dinosaur. The ice dino was carried for a quarter of a mile before being left in a comfortable (and I was told, tasty!) field of grass. The hike in was filled with games of various sorts including I Spy and variations on the Dora the Explorer troll game, where a grumpy troll asks three questions of the various hikers."

Stumping the grownups is immensely appealing to kids this age. Being allowed to ask as many questions as they want is likewise thrilling–although not necessarily to all involved.

In truth, kids this age ask lots of questions, either because they want answers, or because they want attention. Huzzah–you are now in a perfect situation to provide both . . . even though you might be out of range for Googling.

Then again, the kids didn't seem particularly spoiled—especially not on this trip, I thought, as I started handing out the cookies—the whole cookies—to an appreciate audience of small connoisseurs. Our two families, plus additional grown-up friends Tom and Amy, had hiked in to this remote cabin at the hot springs. For the five-year-olds, it was the longest jaunt they'd ever done on their own two feet—and we were expecting them to repeat the accomplishment on the way back out. To the credit of the young adventurers, the amount of whining on the trail was minimal. They were too busy playing "eye spy," carving their names on tree-fungus, asking impossible riddles, and eating vast quantities of snacks. I munched on whatever was left at the bottom of each Ziploc baggie, and I was rarely allotted a chance to declare that, "I spy something beginning with 'S'," but that seemed perfectly normal to all of us.

Why did I set things up this way? Even if a parent-kid inequality doesn't necessarily constitute spoiling, it did seem counter-intuitive that I was teaching my twins to short-change me, when I was so scrupulous about getting them to be fair with one another. When they were barely three, they protested when I handed them five picture books to look at while riding in their bike trailer. "That's not an even number! If I get two, she gets three!" My pride in their math skills surged even as my own crabbiness mounted. I went back inside and grabbed another of Sandra Boyton's semi-indestructible classics off the shelf. See? Everything's even now.

By the time of this hike, they could both tell me that fifty was half of a hundred. When the Easter Bunny brought marbles, they counted every last one of them. They knew what was fair. They knew when someone was getting the short end of the cream-cheese-on-celery-stick. And they knew that, most often, it was me.

In fact, the imbalance was so blatant that it became a joke.

"Here's your share, Mama," one of the kids would chortle, handing me the trimmed-off edges of an art project or the nibbled-down core of an apple. Grinning expectantly, she would wait for me to feign horror at my pathetic portion.

"What?!" That's all I get?"

Giggles. "Yup, that's Mama's share."

Maybe there was something wrong with my brain, because I actually found it kind of funny to be ceremoniously handed a used-up roll of duct tape. Is that a bad sign? Could someone be diagnosed with a martyr complex solely on the basis of their willingness to eat the tough ends of carrots? I knew self-imposed martyrdom tended to be a female problem—and I'd have hated to let my daughters think I was sending the message that "Moms don't deserve the unbroken cookies—or, for that matter, a napkin that hasn't already been used."

But that idea had to be just plain silly. For one thing, the twins were far from miniature sultans in an archaic patriarchy. For another, the grownup male in the household suffered his share of martyrdom too, as did other handy role models. Prior to the Milano dessert course, I'd seen Ned scarf down the congealing remnants of tuna and noodles from around the edges of his own daughter's plate. And Tom didn't bat an eye over the cookie proclamation, even though a) he'd provided half the cookies, b) he was not a parent, and c) he takes his dessert-eating very seriously.

Ok, so I wasn't spoiling my kids out of laziness or conflict aversion. And I wasn't some sort of self-flagellating martyr. Other parents—and even child-free people—were doing this. But what, exactly, was it we were doing?

I recalled what had taken place during our seven hours of hiking—and what, as it happened, would occur again on the way out.

Eight miles into the venture, when my own kids were not-quite-exhausted, their friend hit a wall. Anna collapsed into a sad little heap on the trail, unable to take another step. When Ned heroically hoisted his little girl onto his own tired shoulders, adding forty pounds to the weight of his backpack, I was worried that the twins would rebel and demand equal treatment from Jay and me.

They didn't. Instead, they understood. In a bumbling-novice sort of way, they tried to make allowances.

"She's not as old as we are. She's not in kindergarten yet," they consoled each other, eying their three-months-younger compatriot with kindly (if transparently patronizing) good-humor. "See how tired she is?" They tromped their weary little legs on down the trail.

No doubt, I realized, their friend would soon hand down the same high-minded I'm-so-big attitude toward some hapless four-year-old or cranky toddler. I didn't always remember to give kids credit for all the simultaneous processing their neurons can manage. Just as toddlers can happily become bilingual if exposed to two native tongues, they can also learn two overlapping yet distinct moral codes: be fair . . . but be magnanimous. An important lesson is buried in there somewhere: no matter how little you are, there's always someone out there who's smaller, weaker, or just more in need of a piggyback ride or a whole cookie.

We teach fairness by example, but we teach generosity the same way. Hopefully, as those of us over the age of five consumed our slightly sub-par dessert, we were helping to bolster the ethos that kept the marginally older kids moving past mileposts nine and ten. Fairness is good—but sometimes the right choice is to make oneself content with the metaphorical cookie-crumbs of maturity. What better place to learn this than on the trail?

The sweet taste of success and lollipops brightens spirits on the long hike to Tolovana Hot Springs.
FAMILY PHOTO

But How Do You Deal with . . . Darkness

"Mom, let's take the dogs for a walk."

"Yeah. Okay. They need a walk." I sighed and looked out the window toward where our two mismatched sled dog mutts were snoozing in their straw-filled doghouses. "But it's already dark out there."

"So? We've got headlamps."

My kindergarteners were growing up in a place where "day" and "night" are not concepts closely linked to whether or not the sun

TIP ▪ Headlamps

Headlamps are pretty cheap these days. You can own one. You can own several. You can own one for each kid and extras for when you lose some, and a battery charger full of triple-A's that is constantly getting raided for electronic toys and remote-control helicopters. You can blame each other for depleting the battery supply. But you can all have headlamps.

Nearly all headlamps use LED bulbs these days. Anything else is ridiculous, sucking battery life and wasting it as heat. And even with efficient LEDs, using anything other than rechargeable batteries is likewise frustrating and wasteful. But you'll find tons of choices in terms of size, style, and brightness.

For really long adventures, or anything high-speed, such as biking, you'll want a light with some oomph—most likely a model that takes at least four double-As, or one with a built-in battery that can be charged via USB or other direct plug-in system.

For anything else—hiking, camping, even reading in your tent—a small, light-weight, cheap model that runs on two or three triple-As will be fine. Keep one in your pocket, in your bag, in your car, and pretty much everywhere else.

is above the horizon. My husband grew up in Alaska, too. As for me—well, even after well over a decade, at that point in time, my brain was still trying to catch up with the idea of going out to play in the dark.

Jay, then and now, barely seems to notice whether or not it's light out. His biorhythms don't depend on the path of the sun. On long-distance races, his satellite tracker will move onwards through the dark hours, while I, sleepy at home, can barely keep my eyes open to check it on my laptop.

When they were little, the kids stuck to regular bedtimes and waking times, summer and winter, regardless of whether 7:30 a.m. fell three and a half hours before sunrise, or was merely a seemingly random point in a circle of endless light. Even now, though they sleep a little later on weekends, they seem impervious to light, or the lack thereof.

In my own defense, I feel like I'm the normal one around here. With the exception of extreme circumstances, including the poor choices of literature (see Tip: What Not to Do in the Dark), I've never been particularly afraid of the dark. But at some level, we all are. We're wired that way; we evolved that way. We're diurnal

It's dark. It's cold. 'Mom, can I play outside?'

Probably fifty percent of our dog walks are in complete darkness. Where you would normally have hats, we have an enormous collection of headlamps, flashlights, bike lights, bright lights, lights that need fresh batteries, and so on. Tell yourself, "It's dark, it's cold, and there's no way around it, so I just have to adapt." Staying inside is a very bad option. Instead, buy a ten-dollar headlamp. Tell yourself that darkness and cold are no big deal. If your friends complain, tell them to be quiet. Actually, depends on the friend, but you get my point.

–Lizzy, on the dark realities of sub-Arctic winters

TIP ▪ What Not to Do in the Dark

Swish. Swish. Swish. Rustle. Creak. Rustle. Hoot. WHAT WAS THAT?
Swish. Swish. Swish. Swooping shadows. OMG, WHAT?
If you are skiing alone in pitch darkness with only the shadowy trees and an audiobook for company, don't choose *The Hunger Games*.

---

creatures. Our ancestors invented fire to roast meat and roots and warm caves, but also to keep the darkness at bay.

Alaskan darkness in winter is that kind of ancestral outside-the-cave dark. Not city-light-polluted dark. Not suburban star-gazing dark. Dark dark. I've always been a sci-fi geek, the kind of person who knows how to find Polaris and refers to the moon as a "waning crescent" or "waxing gibbous," but it wasn't until I moved here that I found practical uses for this knowledge—and owned more than one headlamp.

I'm not the only one who finds the illumination fluctuations of this latitude a challenge. For each Fairbanksan who mutters and gripes about temperatures of forty below zero, there's another who is equally cantankerous about days that last for less than four hours. Three hours and forty-one minutes, to be precise.

Yes, we're counting. Yes, everyone at this latitude knows what an equinox is and what a solstice is, and when the next one will occur.

Some poor souls develop full-blown Seasonal Affective Disorder. These folks often have to move to more equitable climes. Many, like me, aren't SAD, but aren't Seasonally Unaffected, either.

Even if you don't live at 64°N latitude, winter days can be short. Darkness is an emotional hurdle. We probably evolved to hunker down near our fires when darkness fell, in order to avoid the sabretooth tigers.

Six-year-old card sharks are unfazed by the dark during tent time in the Grand Canyon. FAMILY PHOTO

Every October, I prop a full-spectrum light next to my desk at work. It keeps me company through February. And, perhaps more importantly, throughout the dark underbelly of the year, I remind myself that playing in the dark is not just okay, it's necessary. And delightful.

Sure, from inside a lighted house, the darkness looks uninviting. But once outside, there's beauty in the night. At worst, there's a trail to be found in a headlight's beam. At best, there are pearlescent shimmering colors dancing across the sky. I've lived here for twenty years, but I still haven't gotten over the aurora, and I don't think I ever will.

Skiing in the dark—sans violent horror stories—can be transcendently peaceful. The narrowed vision to the beam of a headlamp offers focus and perspective. Nocturnal creatures flit, hoot, and howl just out of range. There are owls and wolves and lynx out there, hunting. You will not see them, but you can be a tiny pool of light in their darkness.

In addition, the abundance of darkness teaches us to cherish the light. On the darkest Saturday of the year, I revel in taking part in a deeply crazy but also deeply satisfying event called the Dawn to Dusk Run. The name says it all. Begin running at sunrise, around 11 a.m.—presumably after a generous dose of sleep and a sturdy brunch. Keep running. And running. And running. Return to the basecamp—a cozy space on the University of Alaska campus, fortified with cookies and cocoa—by sunset. Report your GPS-logged miles. That's it. Usually, I manage to cover about seventeen or eighteen miles. Always, my legs are really sore the next day. But as I stagger about, recovering, I am heartened by two facts. First, the days are now getting longer. Second, I have found a way to make the shortest day of the year seem really, really long.

"Come, on, Mom!"

Yeah. The dogs needed a walk. And so did I. Outside we went, to play in the dark.

All dogs love to play outside, but walking the dogs takes on new meaning when the family pets are a motley collection of Alaska sled dogs who love the cold—and love to pull.
FAMILY PHOTO

Seven Miles—with the Logistics of a Hundred

The cozy log shelter known as Lee's Cabin is not a race checkpoint on the White Mountains 100. Any real ultra-racer who is snow-biking, skiing, or running a hundred miles, after all, wouldn't even pause to rip open a Clif bar a mere seven miles into the adventure. And yet two weeks before the big race, Lee's had been not a blip in the background, but the Grand Destination—and I'd spent a lot more time planning for that two-day, fourteen-mile round-trip than for the (theoretically) non-stop hundred-miler.

As I meandered past on my sturdy classic skis during the WM100, I did stop for a moment, and take a good swig from my battered Nalgene of hot chocolate. I felt a little self-conscious for even noticing the cabin's existence, but I could practically hear the echoes of our earlier Spring Break visit.

Lee's Cabin from the Eliot Highway Mile 28 trailhead

Location ▪ White Mountains National Recreation area north of Fairbanks.

Distance and duration ▪ 14 miles round-trip, one overnight.

Locomotion ▪ Cross-country skiing, with adults pulling gear in lightweight plastic pulk sleds.

Terrain ▪ Mixed hills and flats; trail very wide and easy to follow, and packed by previous mushers, skiers, and snowmachiners.

Weather ▪ About 10°F, clear and sunny, typical for mid-March in Fairbanks.

Accommodations ▪ Basic BLM rental cabin equipped with a wood stove (wood gathered by foraging and water melted from snow).

"Two, three, four . . . " The scuffling of ten small hands and an equal number of small feet in the loft of Lee's Cabin had sounded like an infestation of forty-pound squirrels. " . . . seven, eight, nine . . . "

> **TIP ▪ Worst Case Scenarios**
> One challenge inherent to all undertakings involving kids is the need
> to be double-buffered against minor mishaps that would not be
> problematic for adults. Young children are very bad at "just dealing
> with it" if their boots get wet, their sandwich is smushed, or someone
> forgets the Uno cards. If the adventure involves getting your own
> two five-year-olds (not to mention three small people belonging to
> other mommies and daddies) to ski seven miles to a backwoods cabin
> when the temperature is hovering around zero Fahrenheit, make that
> quadruple-buffered. The long-term payback of a happy trip will be
> worth the extra planning and the extra weight.

After several false starts, a total was reached. Down below, the adults
exchanged sardonic glances and waited for the census results to be
announced. The stuffed animal census, that is.

Placing limits on the plush beast population was part of the
elaborate packing process. So was preventing the kids from stuffing
their allotted toy bags with cherished blocks of wood, railroad spikes,
or chunks of granite. Despite these best efforts, the invisible gurus of
Traveling Light mocked me.

"They're all small animals," Lizzy told me earnestly.

I knew that bringing a whole pint of maple syrup—from real
Canadian maple trees!—might be overkill. Then again, running out
of syrup? That would be tragic. I knew that the twins were unlikely
to wear more than one sweater under their snowsuits for the simple
reason that if they did so they'd be unable to move—but what if
one sweater got wet? What if it was accidentally drenched in real
Canadian maple syrup? I brought extras. I worried that the rigors of
the trail, the limitations of a cramped space, or the chill of the cabin
floor might cause my kids to decide that (horrors!) they didn't actually

like ski trips. I countered this eventuality by bringing approximately eight million snacks, plenty of art supplies, slippers, and of course, stuffed animals.

Jay likes to spend whole evenings reading up on the riveting nuances of gossamer-light sleeping bags, tents less hefty than the average guinea pig, stoves that fold into your pocket, and rain jackets that practically levitate. And yet there we were in the woods with not only three boxes of Girl Scout Cookies, eight bedtime stories, and a non-stick non-gossamer frying pan, but also a well-travelled plush Lamby and a toy cat named Dirty Snow. I like to think I know how to prepare for the most extreme of Arctic expeditions, but what I had actually prepared for was a slumber party at which the greatest danger was that someone might wet their sleeping bag or misplace a teddy. The irony stared me in the face with its fuzzy little sewn-on eyes.

Packing for the Whites 100, in contrast, took roughly half an hour. It wasn't that I took the race any less seriously. But I escaped the waiting list and inherited bib #16 only two days before the event—and even then, I couldn't immediately begin stuffing my old blue backpack. I had a few other jobs to do first . . . starting with lining up thirty hours of childcare.

Luckily, our friends are saintly. As far as I know, no one even groaned or rolled their eyes. Still, I had to call upon the collective goodwill of six different long-suffering individuals, each with sleep habits to match their allotted shift. These folks are savvy to the ways of kindergarteners (no unsupervised use of Sharpies; no eating pudding in the living room; beware of scientific experiments involving Silly Putty, food coloring, or grownup scissors), though I still needed to write a few basic instructions about things like pajamas, family doctors, and school schedules. I packed lunch boxes two days in advance, and I packed a canvas bag with enough apples, fishy crackers, cucumber slices, and smoked Gouda to fill the time in between.

As for myself . . . well luckily, there's always plenty of food in our house. Pilot bread? Check. Peanut butter? Crunchy and creamy. I was pretty sure other race participants would be fueled by carefully calibrated rations and high-performance brand-name gels and goos—but there were plenty of those animal cookies left over. I filled two sandwich baggies.

I figured the cookies must be good trail fuel since they'd always been popular with the three-foot-tall skiers. "'Nother cookie, please, Mommy?" The treats were just the right size to stuff into Molly, one at a time, as she struggled along on her Lilliputian skis. No need to take off your mittens when your parent is imitating a bird feeding its fledglings. Look, this one is shaped like a lion! At least, I think that's a lion. Tiger? Endangered snow leopard? Mmmm, chocolatey snow leopard. Keep those skis moving, kiddo!

I kick-waxed my own skis the night before the race in the infinitesimal interval between almost-kids'-bedtime and really-truly-right-now-kids'-bedtime. I tossed the waxes into the top pocket of my backpack, where they fought for space with the headlamp, extra batteries, and small ration of toilet paper.

On the family Spring Break trip, we carried a full medical kid, complete with salves, ointments, and cherry-flavored medications for the kindergarten crowd, just in case. All the necessities. My race backpack had all the medical necessities, too: duct tape wrapped around a pen and six Aleve tablets in a Ziploc. There were four race medics out on the course, and I had a lot of warm clothes. I'd be fine without the Winnie the Pooh Band-Aids.

My slush-proof overboots—for use on the notorious Ice Lakes and other sections of overflow—were actually plastic bags that had once held spruce pellets for our stove. I knew they worked. But I

TIP ▪ Lightweight Toys

Ideally, the correct number of non-essential items to have in your pack would be zero. But that depends on your definition of "ideal" and your definition of "essential." If parents want to maintain their own sanity, they usually find it well worthwhile to let young kids bring along a few carefully selected items for comfort and entertainment. We usually limited this to stuffed animals, card games, and books.

Stuffed animals look ridiculously bulky, but they are usually made of synthetic materials and are very light, so long as you avoid anything with a beanbag filling or heavy plastic parts. They can double as pillows, and even help take up fluffy space in a sleeping bag, making it warmer. And since they are "role-playing" toys, they offer hours of creative play. Teddy is building a house out of sticks! Teddy is eating berries! Teddy is digging a Teddy outhouse!

Little kids are limited in their ability to play complex games, but Uno, memory, and Go Fish offer a lot in terms of entertainment-for-weight ratio.

Picture books are important, but many of them weigh a ton. Hit used books stores and stock up on flimsy paperback ones that don't. (We got a large stash of these free, one by one, in Cheerios boxes, but I suspect that particular promotion ended years ago.)

As mentioned elsewhere, food that doubles as entertainment (animal crackers, cereal necklaces, alphabet cookies, fruit leather art) may not be fair game at home, but on the trail . . . no holds barred.

didn't exactly feel like an ultra-racer with legs that said, "Made from 100% Alaskan Wood."

It was when I was removing this low-rent footwear for the second time in a mile, at about mile ninety-two of the course that a racer on foot caught up with me. Strictly speaking, skiers ought to be far ahead of those who are walking the course, but I knew there were already two foot travelers ahead of me, so my pride wasn't exactly at stake.

In fact, my fellow racer didn't seem scornful of either my slowness or my pellet bags. But I recognized this guy, and I knew that if anyone was a real ultra-racer, he was. Not only has he completed umpteen events, but he was one of only eighteen entrants who actually finished a recent 350-mile ultra, a race that Jay dropped out of after pushing a heavily laden bike through drifts for three days straight. I was very grateful to find that such a supremely accomplished walker was willing to hike the next section of the course with me, because mile ninety-three is Wickersham Wall, a hill just as daunting as it sounds.

And yet, somehow, the Wall wasn't demoralizing at all. I'm not saying I made it up the hill it at lightning speed. I was panting along with my skis strapped to my pack, my knees aching, and my ankles threatening mutiny. But as I chatted with my new friend about his background in theoretical physics, his girlfriend who had snow-biked the course and was (hopefully) awaiting him at the finish, his political frustration and amusement, and his job at Google, it seemed easy to tell him about my kids, my logistical contortions, and my hope that Jay was there at the finish, too. Maybe this guy was a real ultra-racer in a way that I would never be, but he was a real person, too, with a jumbled calendar and competing interests. Moreover, he had a sense of humor—a trait that seems crucial for dealing with not only sleep-deprivation and steep hills, but also PowerPoint presentations, party-catering, small children, and just . . . life, the universe, and everything. Sunshine was pouring down on us, there was still enough afternoon to carry us to the finish line, and we were both having a blast.

The course of the Whites 100 is a loop with a spur at the beginning and end, meaning that I passed Lee's Cabin at mile seven, but also passed within half a mile of it at mile ninety-four, right after topping Wickersham Wall. This time, I was too far away to actually see the cabin, but I gave the left-hand trail a glance and a smile anyhow. I'd be back again. Jay and I would bring the kids back next winter, or perhaps even in the fall, with extra sweaters, chocolate cookies shaped like bison, and plenty of cuddly toys. Maybe we'd even beat 2012's record—although that might be tough.

No, I don't mean we'd beaten the four hours that it took our family of four to cover those seven miles. Who cares about speed? I'm talking about the plush-critter census. When that counting was complete, and the number was relayed down from the loft, even the grownups were impressed. Eighteen stuffed animal companions had made the journey with us.

Stuffed animals are light, packable, can double as pillows . . . and vastly increase morale. FAMILY PHOTO

Have You Seen a Kid and a Puppy? The Beginning of Independence

"Where's Lizzy?"

"Um . . . Ahead somewhere?" Robin, aged thirteen, was standing by the side of the trail, her poles planted and her cross-country skis stationary, apparently contemplating the next section of downhill with some trepidation. She gestured vaguely downslope."

"Oh." I considered this for a moment. "Is Olive with her?"

"I think so?"

The trail out from Stiles Creek Cabin is eight miles long, and very hilly. It winds through spruce and birch forest, taking in some excellent ridgeline views and slightly hair-raising hairpin turns. Like almost all winter trails in the Interior, it is multi-use. One might meet other skiers, mushers, or snowmachiners coming around any of those turns.

"I thought she was with you."

Robin shrugged, slightly sheepish. "It was too steep for me. I took off my skis and walked. But I'm sure she's fine."

Sure. A six-year-old and a puppy were now leading the charge down some of the steepest of those hills. What could possibly go wrong? I peered down the hill and pushed off with my poles.

Stiles Creek Cabin

Location ▪ Chena River Recreation Area, east of Fairbanks.

Distance and duration ▪ 16 miles round trip, with two days of skiing and a rest day in between (two overnights at the cabin).

Locomotion ▪ Cross-country, with kids skiing the full distance and adults hauling gear in pulk sleds.

Terrain ▪ Mostly uphill on the way in, and downhill outbound.

Weather ▪ Clear and sunny spring weather with daytime temperatures above freezing.

Accommodations ▪ Basic DNR rental cabin with wood stove. (Wood gathered and water melted from snow.)

Much as I was worried about my kid, I was also just a little bit thrilled. During almost seven years of Adventure Parenting, I'd done so much waiting. I'd exercised so much patience. I'd so often slowed my pace to an agonizing crawl. This was the first time I'd had to hustle to catch up with a child.

The inbound journey to this cabin had been a prime example of patient plodding. Moving uphill on cross-country skis isn't a rapid endeavor at the best of times, but when three six-year-olds are added to the mix, the word "glacial" become appropriate on several levels. More than once, I had asked myself why we were even bothering with the stupid boards attached to everyone's feet, not to mention the poles that the kids hadn't even properly learned to use. The trail was hard-packed enough to allow for trudging without post-holing. Wouldn't walking be faster?

Eight miles mostly uphill is a long way for young kids. It took us about five hours, which, if you do the math, is . . . not fast. We stopped, we rested, we put skis on an off and on again, we ate snacks, we ate more snacks. The inclusion of an extra friend, Salak, and her adorable puppy, Olive—as well as the teenager and her respective parents—rendered the twins less annoyed by the length and inefficiency of the journey than they otherwise might have been. Plus, it was the very end of March—the blue-sky, perfect-sunshine portion of the Fairbanks winter that would probably attract thousands of tourists if more of them knew how lovely it is. There were no cold fingers or toes, and everyone was tanking up on Vitamin D. Still, it was a long way in. As we labored through it, I was counting on a short way out.

Just maybe not THIS short. Jay and the other adults were behind me, helping to herd the other two kids and manage the awkward sled full of gear hauled by our dogs. On the downhill, it required a brake made of knotted rope, dragging beneath it, so that

"Oh, were you looking for me?" This cross-country skier was unconcerned about getting ahead of the group on the eight mile Stiles Creek Cabin Trail. FAMILY PHOTO

it wouldn't overtake the dogs and slam into them. I was carrying a pack. It wasn't too heavy, but it made it that much harder to control the speed of my descent. I understood Robin's point. Making sharp turns on steep terrain on Nordic skis is not for the faint of heart, especially when the price of an error is plunging headfirst into a snowdrift or a tree.

There was someone ahead of me. Desperately, I snowplowed my skis, torqueing my heels out and my knees in, and digging what edges my skis offered into the hard-packed snow. I ground to a halt only a few feet from a group on foot, walking up the hill. "Um, hi . . ." I paused, "Have you seen a kid and a puppy?"

"A little tiny kid?"

"Uh, yeah. I mean, she's almost seven, actually . . ." Lizzy was small for her age, and crouched over her skis might have passed for a lost kindergartener or younger. I found myself attempting to prove that I wasn't really THAT parent, because, hey, she's in first grade.

"She went flying past. We wondered who she belonged to."

Yeah, okay, I'm that parent.

I hurried down the hill. Another turn, another—sheesh, she'd made those turns without falling? Or maybe not. There was a little wallow-spot in the deep snow. And another. Around one more bend, and there she was, rolling herself out of yet another fall, covered in powder. She was giggling. Olive was frolicking around her, obviously thrilled by this high-speed falling-down game.

"Lizzy! Are you okay?"

She popped to her feet with far more grace than I would have been able to manage and gave me a look. "I'm fine! Where were you?"

"Back with Molly and Salak and everyone. You weren't supposed to be alone . . . "

"Ski with me, Mommy!"

Puppy and child took off downhill once more—and I continued, in their wake.

But How Do You Deal with . . . Potty Breaks in the Woods

Age two or thereabouts is a tricky time for parents, since that's when kids CAN be very reliably potty-trained . . . but aren't necessarily. This is problematic at home, and potentially disastrous in the backcountry. A fully soaked outfit is gross, but a fully soaked insulating sleeping bag on a winter trip is dangerous.

I'll admit here that we had it easy. The twins were born in late May, and by the time winter rolled around when they were two and a half, they could be completely trusted not to wet anything. But results may vary. And regardless of whether your kid is potty-reliable at two or at four, you're still going to need diapers for quite some time.

Diapers are not much fun on outdoor adventures. They're not much fun in any context, of course; being out and about just adds an exciting new level of challenge. All parents already know that you should never, ever leave the house with an infant unless you have a complete set of clothes, at least two more clean diapers than you think you need, and plenty of wipes. Regardless of whether you're using cloth or disposables, you're going to have to carry out whatever your baby soils, so you'll need waterproof bags too. Reliable ones. If it's really cold out, diaper-changing is going to be even worse for everyone involved. But if you have a good setup for keeping your baby warm, the trauma will be reversible. This isn't an issue on a summer jaunt, but you'll hear more about that later.

I'm not, in general, a fan of putting diapers on kids who don't need them. If it's summer, let 'em discover the joys of peeing in the woods, where the WHOLE WORLD is your potty! If they get wet, they get wet. But if it's winter, play it safe.

Playing it safe is even more important if the bodily function in question isn't urination. A few years after the fact, I learned that I'd had the distinct honor of teaching someone else's kindergartener how to poop in the woods. Young Josie credited me with this quite cheerfully, as if it were a real accolade.

And maybe it is. Backwoods bathroom breaks are not glamorous, but they're certainly necessary. And, although someone has managed to write an entire book on the subject, backwoods business isn't actually that complicated. Kids take to it . . . well, naturally.

Peeing in the woods is easy, even if you and/or your kids are female—and even if it's winter. But you'll need to plan carefully.

Do not under any circumstances wear clothes with bibs, suspenders, or complicated fasteners. If you're wearing multiple layers—and you probably will be—this is particularly important. If you can pull down all the layers at once, major bonus.

You can probably keep your cross-country skis on. This is actually easier for kids, assuming they are reasonably comfortable on skis, because they are flexible and have great balance.

If there is deep snow off the trail, do not even try to get far. Common courtesy dictates that all who witness you must pretend that they didn't.

If you have more serious business to deal with, you need to dig a hole. In snow, this is easy, once you overcome the obstacle of trying to get off the trail (see above). In summer months, you'll find that hole-digging is a variable sport. Usually, the easiest burial solution involves moving a fairly large rock (or several), using the hole they leave behind, and then putting the rocks back. At times, when no rocks are available, I've had to lift up sticks and moss and burrow into soft earth with my hands. This tends to leave my hands a bit dirty. But it's a CLEAN dirty. I swear.

As an added note, some adults claim that they have trouble crouching (not something I've ever heard from a kid, because kids are made of rubber). This is obviously a bit of a problem. If you're worried about falling over, or can't get down that far, you may need to find a large rock or a handy tree to cling to, to aid your balance.

Additional caveats are necessary in areas with tight restrictions. You may have to bag up toilet paper, or even waste itself, in areas with high use and low decomposition rates. But on most of our adventures, this issue has been a simple one—and particularly simple for children to learn. Indeed, once you've taught your kids to use the great outdoors as their bathroom, you may find yourself having to deal with the issue of teaching them NOT to do so, in inappropriate contexts.

You Know Your Own Kids

"Hey, please don't shine your headlamps over here!"

Jay's voice was disembodied in the blackness. He'd obviously turned off his own light, allowing the moonless canyon to swallow him whole. For a moment I wondered what nefarious activity could possibly require such absolute privacy. Then he added, "I'm taking photos of the stars."

Photos. Of the stars.

The red sprawling glow of monstrous, dying Betelguese was clearly distinguishable from white-hot triple-stellate Rigel in the tilted outline of Orion— unsullied by the distant glow of diffused neon and insistent headlights. Our tent, insignificant and alone, was staked in sand previously imprinted by the heavy paw of a mountain lion. The tent rippled in the dust-dry breeze of New Year's Eve.

This was not what I'd expected.

Nearly five million people visit the Grand Canyon each year.

The Grand Canyon

Location ▪ Grand Canyon National Park, South Kaibab and Bright Angel trails, with a short section of the Tonto Trail.

Distance and duration ▪ Five days: two days to hike down, two days to hike up, and one day of day-hiking near the bottom in between.

Locomotion ▪ Hiking, with kids hiking the full distance and adults carrying all the gear..

Terrain ▪ Continuously hilly but never steep or tricky, with a very wide trail.

Weather ▪ Clear and sunny January weather, about 25°F at night and 40s or 50s during the day.

Accommodations ▪ Tent camping, both backcountry and at designated campgrounds. Drinking water limited, but available. A few snacks and other items can be purchased at Phantom Ranch at the bottom of the canyon.

Small hikers had no problem navigating a big canyon on a family vacation to Arizona. FAMILY PHOTO

That, for the numbers-challenged, is . . . a lot of people. As in about seven times the population of the state of Alaska.

I'm no misanthrope, and I don't (yet) share Jay's opinion that all regions south of the 50th latitudinal parallel are deeply suspect and over-subscribed by humanity. And still, when I'd booked our "backcountry" itinerary—months in advance, per Park Service advice, in order to wrangle with thousands of presumed competitors for our tent spots—I'd had my misgivings

I fervently hoped that most of the five million would never leave the Canyon rim ("Gosh, how lovely, now we can buy knick-knacks and cross this off our bucket list!"). There was also the question of mules. How wild could this place be, if the trails are traipsed daily by four-legged big-eared cross-bred copiously-pooping equines? Based on websites and hearsay, I imagined the sort of camping that involves Ranger Tess (who wears a comical hat and provides Informative Lectures about Wildlife); or Rhonda and Al from Cleveland (who have grandkids just about the twins' age, would you like to see photos?); or Unprepared Bill (who wonders if maybe you have some spare fuel, and manages a snore so impressive that it can be heard from the next Designated Tent Site).

Don't get me wrong, I like Ranger Tess, Rhonda, Al, and Bill. I'm moderately gregarious (even if socially maladroit), and meeting other campers offers me a chance to turn them into fictional characters at some future date. Besides—gratifyingly, if mysteriously—they always seem to dote on my kids. When I booked the Family Vacation, I was hoping (with the blind optimism of all such bookings) to have fun, create great memories, and dodge disaster. Two adults, two six-year-olds, five Alaska Airlines flights, a rental car in a vast and unfamiliar city, promises of accommodation from friends who tolerated me two decades ago, and a six-day camping permit for a place I'd never set eyes on—what could possibly go wrong? Ok, so I was expecting a lot. But whatever I was expecting from the Grand Canyon, it wasn't a True Wilderness Experience.

As a long-time official (and unofficial) environmentalist, I've been privy to a few too many conversations about the Meaning of Wilderness. Particularly in Alaska, wilderness is an issue of politics, and ethics, and economics. Does wilderness preclude all sight or sound of humans? Is it sustainable? Is setting aside "untouchable" land culturally inappropriate, with respect to Indigenous peoples? Is our adulation of wilderness a blind glorification of a less-than-glorious and perhaps mythical past? Is it essentially nihilistic? And can it possibly occur in a popular National Park, a mere few hundred feet from an established trail?

It seemed improbable. But here, tweaked by latitude, were our own winking Alaska stars, as we'd seen from remote and uncompromising outposts such as Windy Gap or Tolovana. For the first time in a long time, I was experiencing early-evening darkness without skis, or snowdrifts, or temperatures cold enough to make my nostrils crackle. After playing Uno and building rock-forts for teddy bears amidst the prickly pear, I could point out to my kids the fine-scale detail of the scabbard at the Hunter's hip (and then I could define "scabbard"). What could be more pleasing to a backcountry nerd?

> A common question was, "What if they fall off?" Everyone knows their kid. However, I have to say, even though six-year-olds have bad judgement, no six-year-old is going to jump into the Grand Canyon. The possibility that they would accidentally fall in is close to zero. Before stressing about something, ask yourself, would I even be tempted to do that? If you can easily answer that in less than ten seconds, chances are that your kid will have the sense or instincts not to do it.
> —*Lizzy, advocating for the trustworthiness of six-year-olds*

And yet, this joy of isolation was only a counterpoint, and not a contrast, to the more social and civilized portions of our pleasant six day jaunt. Thus far, everything had gone swimmingly. Our flights were on time. Our baggage showed up. The rental car was not an Edsel, and Google Maps calmly talked us out of Phoenix. ("The robot never gets mad when you miss the turn," noted Molly. I can't imagine to whom she might be comparing said robot). Our brief stay in Flagstaff with my college friend David and his family could not have been more perfect. Hospitality and good company are a boon in and of themselves, but did we really deserve perfect sunshine, a tour of the city, a hot tub, and kids precisely aged to match ours?

The early riser is already busy. An ultra-light three-person tent was still large enough for the four of us at this point. FAMILY PHOTO

Even when we arrived at our destination to discover that our entire camping itinerary had been derailed by a snow closure on Hermit Road . . . it was all ok. I shuffled into the Backcountry Information Office mentally cursing Arizona for spiraling into panic over a mere dusting of the white stuff, but within five minutes, a charmingly cavalier young ranger arranged for new campsites. It seemed things were not as all-booked-up-three-months-in-advance as direly predicted. He also granted us a couple of nights of "at large" camping.

I liked that phrase, "at large," because it felt slightly dangerous and on-the-lam. Watch out, world! Frescos and Cables at large! I didn't dream, though, that we would be as "at large" as this. I knew we didn't have the whole canyon to ourselves. We certainly didn't hold title to the whole wheeling cosmos. Still, even if wilderness is a human construct born of smoke-and-mirrors idealism, I relished the illusion.

But I also, as it turned out, relished our evenings at Bright Angel and Indian Garden. I happily helped the kids pluck grass to feed to over-eager big-lipped mules in their dirt-trodden pen. I enjoyed watching the twins eagerly yet laboriously print missives on oversize postcards while sipping lemonade at Phantom Ranch. I liked the blunt and gregarious ranger who told us, "Kids are never the problem; it's the fat guys who 'did this no problem twenty years ago' who have heart attacks down here." I laughed at the fact that the campground and the nadir of the Grand Canyon offered heated bathrooms with flush toilets, putting our own frigid outhouse to shame.

I even, perversely, enjoyed all the people who stared at the kids and then asked us questions that barely veiled their horror. Like my parents, who had visited the Grand Canyon a decade and a half ago, they seemed a mite worried about . . . cliffs. Also edges, drop-offs, vast precipices, and the conjunction thereof with Very Precious Children. Throughout the trip, we encountered people who clearly thought we were irresponsible nut-jobs, but were too polite to couch it in exactly those terms. I'm not particularly afraid of heights myself, and I have a fair bit on confidence in the self-preservation instincts of my offspring, but I can't help being endeared to anyone who thinks my children are worthy of protection. A few years ago, I might have worn the Bad Parent badge with greater unease, but many other adventures—including Five-Month-Old Twins Go Winter Camping! and Four-Year-Olds Love the Chilkoot!—broke me in nicely.

I was also amused by the now-familiar refrain of, "You're making your kids walk how far? Over what? And sleep where?" I hereby maintain that little kids will gladly walk all day long, if 1) they don't realize that they can't; 2) you really, really like playing Eye Spy; and 3) you provide enough lollipops. Having lots of mule poop to examine is a total bonus. If we only saw one other smallish child in six days (we borrowed her for Uno), it was not because of "can't" but because of "won't." But it just meant more smotherings of adult attention for our two. They enjoyed it, and so did I.

And, interspersed with all this camaraderie, I also enjoyed—deeply, achingly—that moment when the stars deigned to have their pictures taken.

Jay showed me his photo attempts. The distant suns showed up with startling clarity, even on the dim little screen. "That's just thirty seconds. When I tried a really long exposure I got blurring," he said. "All the stars looked like little lines."

I smiled into the darkness. "Because the earth is turning," I said.

The earth was turning in the star-speckled darkness, with all of us on it. I couldn't explain why that made me so happy, and I couldn't say we had found real wilderness. But ultimately, I decided, did those definitions really matter? Maybe wilderness—or just "wildness," if you prefer—is at least partially subjective. Perhaps it is something to be savored in small doses, like the "naughty" foods on the USDA nutrition charts, lest we become dulled to its charms. I knew I would not have enjoyed this moment as much without the other moments, the Junior-Ranger-Badge-earning moments, the loaning-someone-our-cooking-pot moments. Wildness is as multi-layered as the canyon itself, and can be enjoyed best when you dip down, then up, then down again across its crazy landscape.

On the very edge of a new year, there we were: the four of us, plus sundry stuffed animals . . . at large. Sunset had long since lingered, reddened, and winked out from the red-green-brown layers of the jagged, looming walls. The voltage of thirteen alkaline batteries was all that lay between us and the blackness. We'd walked scarcely two miles off the mule-beaten track, past the chest-high cairns that marked the official edge of wilderness. And yet we had the night, the canyon, the whole universe, it seemed, to ourselves. And Orion was winking at us.

But How Do You Deal with . . . Bugs

"Mosquitoes are important because they pollinate the blueberries," Lizzy, aged five, told me, "and they're food for dragonflies and spiders."

Maybe I shouldn't have read them Charlotte's Web. Nonetheless, I abetted the educational experience, and told the kids that only the girl mosquitoes bite. (The boys sip nectar, presumably while singing kumbaya). A quick Google search revealed those hungry *Aedes* ladies can find us by following our CO_2 upstream from a hundred feet away. Once they get close, they are also attracted to body heat and body scent.

My scent in particular, apparently. Since I doubt that I am a particularly heavy breather, I have to assume that I excel in the other two categories. I am indeed a very warm person. This is handy in Alaska in January, but not so handy in June. All that hot blood rushing around in my surface capillaries, coupled with my apparently irremovable human-stink, makes me irresistible. Mosquitos are the insect world's forsaken, and I am their goddess.

Mosquito protection (and also protection from black flies, no-see-ums, and other small creatures who wish to chew your flesh and suck your blood) is kind of a Big Deal in Alaska. Getting bitten can not only make you itch, it can also make you sick—or make you flat-out insane.

Different people have different needs when it comes to insect protection, depending on how sensitive they are, how toxin-averse they are, and how tasty they are. Some people swear by DEET. On the plus side, it works. On the downside, it's nasty stuff. I don't put it on myself, and I definitely wouldn't put it on a kid. (Think about what ends up in kids' mouths . . .).

Less toxic chemicals work, too, to varying degrees. They smell, to varying degrees. And they wear off quickly, to varying degrees. I like Picaridin, but choosing what you can best tolerate can be a process of testing and elimination.

Raw cloves of garlic didn't help me much, but gave me a fascinating coating on my tongue. What about limiting how much carbon dioxide I release? For brief stops such as shoe-tying or peeing, waiting to exhale really does seem to help—or maybe it's just that the lack of oxygen makes me delusional. Have you ever tried to change a bike tire while holding your breath and trying not to sweat? Desperate people do desperate things.

What really works is outracing the insects, or hiding from them. Head nets are awkward and hot, but they are cheap, light, easy, and a small price for not losing your mind. I can usually get by with non-toxic bug-dope while I'm in motion. When I stop, on go the long sleeves and the net.

When the twins were babies and toddlers, we used giant nets that fit over the whole carrier. I sewed these myself by creating a seam around the edge of a circle of netting, threading elastic through it, and adding a toggle. If you don't feel like firing up a sewing machine, take heart: my thought was not as original as I imagined. You can buy such things online.

"How fast can mosquitoes, fly, exactly?" I mused to a friend one day when the kids were little. We were idling at a playground, leaning on the primary-colored tubes and bars.

"One and a half miles per hour." The answer came, instantaneously, not from a fellow adult, but from a snub-nosed child who had just popped his head out of a plastic tunnel. Eight years old, I guessed. He didn't wait for confirmation or thanks before disappearing down the slide, his face earnest, his hair sticking up from static electricity. I liked his answer (and when I looked it up later, it turned out he was right). It set the bar easily within reach. Even preschoolers ought to be able to move that fast.

Not that I was able to keep up the pace when I was a preschooler myself. One of my first memories of backwoods hiking was climbing a mountain called Ampersand, a

One of my favorite memories of mosquitoes is when we were hiking along the Alaska Pipeline, and we woke up and found that our tent wall between screen and fly was a solid wall of bugs, filling the tent with a hypnotic buzzing.

Later, when we set out with backpacks all packed, I got out one piece of really valued clothing: a bug shirt. But the real glee was that Dad had no bug shirt, no head net, and was wearing shorts–and was a perfect target for gloating.
–*Lizzy, on the joys of being better prepared than your parents*

nice rocky little peak in the Adirondacks, whose only drawback was a rather boggy stretch near the trailhead. This was 1977, and I believe I was wearing plaid bell-bottoms, meaning my legs, thankfully, were covered. My hair, however, was pulled up into two crooked pigtails. By that evening, the welts were so thick on my neck that I looked as if I had a combination of mumps and goiters. I couldn't move my head in any direction. My mother, consumed by parental guilt that I only now understand, insisted that on subsequent hikes that summer I wear a peculiar headdress made from an old t-shirt soaked in citronella.

Weirdly, though, I decided I liked hiking. I was thrilled by hiking. It was just the biting insects I despised. Over the next dozen years, I begged to hike more peaks—in Maine, Vermont, upstate New York, and other vermin-infested locales. I got a summer job working on the Adirondack Trail Crew, a job composed of equal parts mud, bugs, and bravado. By the time I was halfway through college, I was well seasoned in the woods. I was also quick to smack mosquitoes and black flies the second they landed on me—to the consternation of my friend Steve, who knew me to be a both pacifist and a vegetarian.

But who was he to talk? The insects always seemed to leave him alone.

Ages 7–9:
We Want a Vote
in This

Their Own People

In this age range, it's still a good bet that your kids will be a lot smaller and weaker than you are—but don't let that fool you. Second-through fourth-graders are tough, wiry, flexible, tenacious creatures. Their legs have, thankfully, gotten a lot longer, and so have their attention spans. If they've been outdoor adventurers since birth, by this stage they will be old hands—packing gear, planning their own snacks, and persuading friends that this is all a Very Good Idea. On the flip side, they will also have developed more complex opinions, and a more elaborate vocabulary with which to inform you that you planned your trip entirely wrong.

If the event you go to the local animal shelter to pick out a new canine family member, your seven-year-olds will not only tag along, they will also retain complete veto power over any decisions. They will name the new pet, most likely after a dog in a kids' book. You will not get a say in the matter. On the plus side, you really can expect them to take care of the new companion. They're old enough for that.

This is the age range in which kids can sometimes do things on their own. Like, completely on their own. No, I don't suggest a free-range-kids Iditarod, but a kids-only bike ride to the local park or a child-powered walk to the nearest store is—current anxious mores notwithstanding—pretty awesome.

The Joys and Perils of Not Being in a Car

"I promise I'm not trying to be a pain. We do this almost every year."

The reservation agent at the other end of the phone line sounded dubious, anxious, and young. I knew that he was not in Alaska, and had most likely never been here. "Those are the rules," he told me firmly. "If you're not driving your own vehicle to Teklanika, you can stay for less than three days, but you have to buy camper bus tickets."

But . . . we started doing this way back when the kids were five: riding, with them doing their very best to add power on their tag-alongs, on the thirty mostly uphill miles to Teklanika Campground. We'd done it again and again.

Denali National Park Entrance to the Passes

Location ▪ Denali National Park.

Distance and duration ▪ Three days, for a total of about 80 miles.

Locomotion ▪ Biking, with kids on tag-along bikes behind adults and gear in panniers.

Terrain ▪ Hilly, some paved road but mostly gravel.

Weather ▪ Mixed sun and rain, variable summer weather 55–75°F.

Accommodations ▪ Tent camping at Teklanika Campground (camp sites with outhouses, drinking water, bear-safe lockers).

I recall thinking they twins would never want to make the trip again, after the wet ride they endured before they'd even started kindergarten. Would they recall, with horror, having to wear sunglasses in the rain in order to keep the mud from fountaining into their eyes? Would they have flashbacks to how, having finally finished the slog, I desperately attempted to sponge them off in the Visitor Center women's bathroom, where the water ran ice-cold and the other guests, fresh from well-appointed camper-vans, looked away from the crazy people with studied nonchalance? And yet, when the twins were seven, they were more than game to hop on the bikes and do the ride again.

We'd gotten smart, in the intervening years, and had added fenders, to both our own rear wheels and the tag-alongs themselves. The weather was marginally better this time—a bit misty and drizzly here and there, but not a mud-fest. Still, it was still almost entirely uphill for the first half of the thirty-mile ride. No propitious weather forecast will ever change that fact.

It would be uphill again this year, I thought, as I explained, once again, that we would not be taking the bus, because we'd be riding our bikes. As we always did. "Bikes are allowed anywhere on the Park Road," I explained. "You probably just haven't dealt with this kind of reservation before, because not many visitors do this."

I was trying to be polite, but I was also telling the truth: they don't. The few bikers we've seen over the years are usually either day-tripping near the Park entrance or near Teklanika campground, or (more adventurously) day-tripping further into the Park, and taking advantage of the fact that one can, in fact, squeeze a bike on a camper bus. It might be a fun way to hopscotch about, but not with more than two bikes—and definitely not with two bikes with tag-alongs attached.

We didn't go unnoticed on that trip when the twins were seven. Soon after we rolled into Teklanika Campground and started setting up camp, I saw there were a couple of kids—boys significantly older than our two—circling the dirt road again and again. They peered at us covertly. We tried to say hi, but they skittered away shyly. I figured they'd come from one of the campers, though I was wrong.

Not long after, a friendly woman approached our spot and introduced herself as the campground host. Behind her, like awkwardly large ducklings, came the two boys. Her sons. They were encumbered—one with a whole bundle of firewood, and the other with a grocery bag. Our kindly host explained, as the boys put down their burdens, that she felt that any family that rode bicycles all the way to Teklanika deserved some s'mores.

Molly and Lizzy, needless to say, were enchanted. And the correlation was formed in their seven-year-old brains: ride bikes. People will be impressed. Then, s'mores!

"Yes, that's fine." When I started to feel that I was unduly stressing out the poor young man on the phone, I thanked him kindly, hung up, and redialed the same number.

The next random-chance reservation specialist I talked to may or may not have dealt with Park Road cyclists before, but she accepted my explanation. I made my reservations. In a few weeks, we'd be back on the bikes. This time heading even further, to Wonder Lake at mile eighty-five.

Letting Kids Get Dirty

"Mommy? Is it ok if I get my pants muddy?"

I looked down at Molly. She and her sister were splashing at the silty edge of the Chena River. There was mud oozing through the mint-green holes in her Crocs, mud caked in a ring around the bottom of her pants, and mud on her arms up to the elbow. By normal standards, her question had come a little late. But I knew what she meant. "Go for it," I told her.

"Yes!" Molly let out a happy-kid noise, and just in case her twin didn't hear the good news, she passed it on: "We can get dirty!" And both children immediately plunged waist-deep into the dense brown muck.

Sometimes a little sunshine and a local water body—such as the Chena River in downtown Fairbanks—provide all the muddy adventure you need. FAMILY PHOTO

Part of me sighed inwardly. Letting kids get dirty—really dirty, as dirty as they want to be—is not without consequences. Those consequences are not only logistical, but also social. Filthy children earn odd looks from strangers—or, even worse, non-looks. You know what I mean: a brief and scuttling glance, followed by a fixed blindness to sights simply too vile and offensive to exist in polite society.

This is no minor taboo. Americans are clean folks. A New York Times article from 2010 starts with the lead, "A daily shower is a deeply ingrained American habit. Most people would no sooner disclose they had not showered in days than admit infidelity."

Our culture is so squeamish about being "dirty" that we don't necessarily clarify whether that means the same thing as being "covered with dirt"—which my children, at that moment on the shores of the Chena, indubitably were. Dirt and dirtiness are related, of course—and yet also peculiarly distinct. As far as I can tell, there are several fundamentally different reasons why we wash things. These include health (influenza is bad; cholera is really really bad); odor (Americans have declared a war on armpits); comfort (wow, these sheets feel nice without all the crumbs); visual aesthetics (no, Lizzy, you can't save that ice cream on your chin for later); and a combination of social pressure and cultural habit (I can't go out, I haven't taken even taken a shower!).

Let's take them in order: health. That's easy; I'm . . . wait for it . . . in favor of it! Yay, health! I get annual flu shots and the recommended number of physicals, and I vaccinate my kids. I try to keep everyone's immune system in top shape through consumption of blueberries, brown rice, and chard; plenty of sleep; and vigorous bike-riding, wrestling, and duck-duck-goose. I encourage lots of hand-washing. I avoid contact with plague-bearing fleas, and I generally eschew exchanging bodily fluids with strangers.

Moreover, I'm an avid rinser of the type of dirt more precisely termed "super-nasty-chemicals-that-we-insist-on-spraying-on-stuff." These, like *Yersinia pestis* bacteria, aren't usually visible. Nevertheless, they come conveniently ready-applied to our fruit and pre-injected into our farm animals. How handy! These toxins (which to me seem like the ultimate in "dirtiness") seem to show up in a lot of our cleaners, probably because anything designed to obliterate germs tends to be iffy for your own body, too. I'm careful (but not always consistent, and certainly not obsessive, because who has the energy to be either consistent or obsessive?) about avoiding that kind of dirt—the kind that no one thinks of as "dirt". Heck, I don't even use mosquito repellant with DEET in it. And I live in Alaska.

Speaking of mosquitoes, let's move on to "comfort." Well, I'm in favor of comfort, too—but my views on what is delightfully cushy don't always seem to mesh very well with other people's opinions. In my world, grimy sandals held together with duct tape are extraordinarily comfortable, as are my marginally stained t-shirt and pair of shorts, on their third or fourth or maybe seventh wearing since they last rolled around in the washing machine. The smear of bike grease on my leg and the trace of ketchup on my elbow count as comfortable too, given that I've forgotten about them. Stiff new shoes and buttoned-up cleanliness not so much.

Most adults seem to take it as a given that being wet or messy is uncomfortable. But I suspect that this is a learned discomfort, rather than an intrinsic one. Small children make great bellwethers, since they are hyper-sensitive (read: scream like banshees) in response to the smallest boo-boo. They will do their very best to reach their 117-decibel potential if they are too cold, stung by a bee, or forced to wear an itchy sweater. However, they don't much care about being either a little sweaty or even dripping with the stuff. So long as they are not chilly, they also don't mind being rain-damp, or full-on head-to-toe sloshing-with-every-movement rain-soaked. Mud? Grime? An upended jar of honey? The more the better! They will happily wiggle their hands into the Play-Doh, plunge their arms into the wet sand, and hurl their whole exhilarated bodies into a swamp.

Which is, of course, exactly what my kids were doing on the banks of the flooded Chena. We were, at that moment, eight miles from home, with only our trusty tandem Trail-a-Bike as transportation. Whatever degree of filth and moisture the kids accumulated, they would be wearing, publicly, all across town. I, of course, would be branded as The Mom Who Let Her Kids Go Out Like That.

Which bring us to "social norms." I do worry about Being A Social Freak. I think by this point word was already out that if you dropped off your innocent child for a playdate under my care, they would be returned with mud stains, grass stains, blueberry stains, and weird stains of unknown origin. You might find, for example,

> ### TIP ▪ Playing with Fire
>
> For older kids, being allowed to do things that seem daring, adult, and a little dangerous is a huge draw. Playing with dirt and water are great, but playing with fire is even more alluring.
>
> The good news is that outdoor adventures offer great opportunities to play with fire in ways that are safe, or at least safe-ish. Axes, saws, and matches must always be used with caution, and forest fires are a hazard to be avoided at all costs, but fires built with adult supervision on gravel bars, in designated spots, or in carefully made rings of rocks can all provide hours of entertainment. And s'mores, of course.
>
> Knowing how to gather kindling, cut and split wood, and start a fire from scratch under any and all conditions is a fabulous life skill.
>
> If it can also be a game, all the better.

that when she got into your tidy family car, her shorts were muddy and soaking wet. There might be twigs in her hair. On one notable occasion, over the course of about five hours, I managed to transform two perfectly respectable and fully clothed kids, then aged six and ten, into feral shirtless creatures streaked with dirt, fermented wild-cranberry war-paint, and dried blood.

Yes, this can occur in the space of time that it takes you to enjoy a movie and shop for some new patio furniture—because, okay, I really am The Mom Who Lets Kids Do That.

I am also The Mom Who Remembers Being That Kid. There's a correlation, I'm sure. My own mother told me stories about her early childhood, which—despite being somewhat lacking in store-bought toys, due to the wallop Great Britain took in WWII—was apparently rich in entertainment. Did you know that sweet little

English girls back in the 1940s enjoyed chasing each other around idyllic, bucolic fields, and throwing partially dried patties of cow poop at one another? Well, now you do. Perhaps not surprisingly, my mother often happily allowed her own daughters to be Those Kids.

As I got older, though, I recall feeling a vague pressure to start being cleaner. Big kids—especially big girls—were supposed to start living by some of the grownup rules that included daily showers, deodorant, and a distaste for spiders, caterpillars, and competitively spat watermelon seeds.

I never quite managed this transformation. (You're shocked.) Oh, some things changed. I stopped wandering around with chocolate ice cream on my chin, and I tried not to pick my scabs or my nose in public. But I never fully internalized the repugnance toward the stuff our whole planet is made of—namely, dirt.

And then, thank goodness, I found summer employment doing trail repair—first, in high school, with the Student Conservation Association, and then in college with the Adirondack Mountain Club. As a member of a trail crew, being dirty—being REALLY dirty—wasn't just a matter of course, it was a matter of provenance. We were foul. We were encrusted. We were so dirty that we were banned from the Lake Placid Laundromat for fouling their washers, and had to take to presoaking our clothes in the lake. My summers were, in short, delightful.

I couldn't remain forever in a time-machine College Summer, but moving to Alaska was the next best thing. Watching my kids cavort in the Chena, even knowing that we'd be sloshing our way home, I still felt like less of a pariah than I would have if we'd been about to board a Long Island Railway train full of people reading the New York Times and pretending not to be able to see me.

Of people like me, the Times has this to say: "Resist the urge to recoil at this swath of society: They may be on to something. Of late, researchers have discovered that just as the gut contains good bacteria that help it run more efficiently, so does our skin brim with beneficial germs that we might not want to wash down the drain."

Good to know. My bacteria-friends and I get along pretty well. Still, I'm feeling a bit sensitive about your use of the word "recoil."

Even as I worry about how I may be judged, I know that telling me to stay squeaky clean all the time—well, it seems about as viable a notion as telling a goldfish to stay dry. Gardening involves dirt. Chopping firewood is not neat. Hiking through a forest, canoeing down a river, and biking a trail are not sweat-free and fully sanitized activities. Earth, soil, worms, dogs, joy, connection, exploration, living in general—none of these things are anything like a blue Windex sheen on a polished surface. And yes, America, having kids is not tidy, either. Not at any stage in the process.

I glanced at my own kids, splashing with delight in the murky water—then looked again. I was pretty sure I only had twins, but now there were three of them. A round-faced little boy, slightly smaller than my two, had sprouted from out of nowhere and joined the fun. As I watched, he gazed admiringly at his role models—my filthy, filthy, daughters. As I watched, he precisely copied Molly's mud-ball-forming technique. As I watched, one of his legs sank gleefully knee-deep.

"Tyler! Tyler!" (Not his real name, because I can't remember his real name). From the park plaza above, I heard the distinct call of a mother hen who had lost her chick. Her voice was not yet worried, but was thinking about being worried.

"He's down here," I called, not without some trepidation. He's down here, and I've ruined him.

Within seconds, both of Tyler's parents ambled into view. They looked at their kid. I looked at them. I saw, from the mom-person, a slight grimace. But the dad was now watching Molly, who was bent over and digging rapidly and assuredly, like a puppy, making a fortification out of a huge heap of mud. Then he looked at Lizzy, her pigtails flying half loose, her jeans sodden, and some unknown substance caked on one side of her face. Finally, he glanced at me. I wasn't precisely IN the mud, but, then again, my sandals were neither clean nor dry.

Tyler's dad grinned enormously. "He's found friends," he said.

The Many Stages of Biking

Molly and Lizzy learned to ride bikes without training wheels just after their fourth birthday. Whee! But it didn't occur to me until the kids got much older that there would be so much overlap between the time during which they have been fully independent bikers and the time during which it still makes sense to pedal with them.

I'm pretty sure we're still remembered around town as the family that had the three-person bike.

When the twins started to get to be too big for the bike trailer, I was anxious to maintain my crazy-bike-person lifestyle. A tag-along bike—a kid-powered bike featuring a single wheel and a long arm to connect to the adult's seat post—seemed like a great option. I saw people using them around town, and friends assured me that kids aged four to seven loved pedaling with Mom or Dad. But . . . I had TWO four-year-olds.

We don't live in Amsterdam, meaning that the options for amazing multi-kid bike contraptions were somewhat limited. After online research, however, I found one company, Adams, that made a tandem trail-behind. I found one store that was willing to ship. I won't name them, because I think that after honoring their deal, they quickly closed the free-shipping-anywhere-in-the-US loophole. Alaska IS in the US, but . . . yeah.

These bikes are great for boosting enthusiasm and independence, but they're definitely not designed for long-distance touring. FAMILY PHOTO

For family adventures, we used two ordinary one-child tag-alongs, handed down from friends. For the many jaunts around town during which it was just me, Molly, and Lizzy, we played the part of the Awesome Threesome on our marvelous machine. We looked unusual, to say the least, but we got our money's worth—and a lot of friendly waves.

We now own two tandem bikes. Like our other gear, we found these second-hand, but they were still a bit of an investment. Still, they are completely worth it. In fact, two other friendly families, seeing the fun we've been having, have made similar purchases.

It's not that the twins can't bike a long way on their own. They willingly set off on private adventures that involve twenty-five-mile days, all over town. But fifty-plus mile days are a bit much to ask,

This unusual double attachment, by Adams Trail-a-Bike, provided triple pedal power—and allowed us to get around town in style. FAMILY PHOTO

and we've only just reached the stage at which their personal bikes have wheels as large as those of adults. It's hard for even big kids to keep up if they are spinning twenty-inch or even twenty-four-inch wheels, and the ratio of rider-weight to bike-weight sets them at a disadvantage. Tandems offer high-speed efficiency and a chance to chat as we cruise along.

But How Do You Deal with . . . Kids in Boats

I'm not much of a boater, so water-borne vessels don't feature heavily in these pages. That doesn't mean they haven't sometimes featured in our lives. With very young children, boats can be a great way to bypass all the hassle of lugging. You can carry a lot more weight in a canoe than you can on your back.

In all such ventures, lifejackets are obligatory, obviously. Other safety considerations include planning for worst case scenarios, in which everyone gets very wet and (inevitably) very cold. Dry-bags with a complete change of clothes are a must. If you are in a remote area, you might need to immediately start a fire or put cold children in sleeping bags. Icy water is no joke, and Alaska rivers are never exactly balmy, even in late summer.

While you might not want to be trapped in a tiny boat with an active toddler for hour after hour, and while you might want to avoid risky whitewater, a float downriver (on the Chena River, for example, which flows conveniently right through Fairbanks) or a cross-lake adventure (for example at nearby Chena Lakes) can be good splashy fun.

As kids get older, they can take an active role in paddling, rowing, and steering. At the age of nine, the twins and their friend Emma wobbled around Chena Lakes in their own canoe, seeking new shorelines and arguing about who was screwing up the steering.

Packrafting required more expensive gear, though loaner boats may be available. It also requires more elaborate trip planning. But even if it happens to hail—more about that later—it's worth it.

Canoeing, kayaking, or rafting can offer outdoor fun for all ages. Conveniently, the Chena River runs right through the heart of Fairbanks. FAMILY PHOTO

The Ups and Downs of Bicycle Tourism

"Mama, this is not fun."

The voice from behind me was thin and high, almost lost in the headwind that my young co-pedaler and I had been battling, mile after mile. It was, nonetheless, quite firm. "This is not fun!"

Guilt stabbed at me. The twins, aged seven, did not sign up for this. And, let's face it, Lizzy had a point. Normal tourists rent cars.

The insistent 48°F rain blew up the cuffs of my raincoat. It spun from my front wheel and dripped from my panniers. It trickled off the end of my nose. It had been raining—or drizzling, or splattering, or heavily misting—all day. We had likewise been treated to almost unceasing precipitation all of the previous day, as we had struggled against a headwind on the road from Hólaskógur to Brautarholt. The day before that, between Flúðir and Hólaskógur—it rained. Chilly, grey, slanting moisture. I wasn't holding out for anything better in Eyrarbakki and Stokkseyri.

Bike Touring in Iceland

Location ▪ Western Iceland, starting from Keklavik Airport and visiting waterfalls, geysers, Reykjavik, and other points of interest.

Distance and duration ▪ Two weeks, covering about 25-50 miles per day.

Locomotion ▪ Biking, with kids on tag-along bikes behind adults and gear in pannier bags.

Terrain ▪ Varied, from flat to steep hills. Road shoulders sometimes narrow.

Weather ▪ Mixed sun and rain, variable summer weather 55-75°F.

Accommodations ▪ About a third of the days clear and sunny with highs around 70°F. Otherwise, rain varying from light drizzle to fairy heavy, with sometimes extreme winds.

Family vacation, 2013. Gosh, kids, let's go bike touring and tent camping! In . . . (wait for it) . . . Iceland!

Our group included Jay, Molly and Lizzy, myself, and Tom (who is in no way related to us by blood, but is so strangely tolerant of our company that he came along on this questionable family vacation). Our Grand Scheme was that as a getaway from our home in remote, Subarctic, sparsely populated Alaska, we would visit a remote, Subarctic, and sparsely populated nation with place names such as "Kirkjubæjarklaustur" and "Fáskrúðsfjörður"; local delicacies such as fermented shark and smoked puffin; and summer weather marked by chilly temperatures, heavy rain, high winds, and rampant unpredictability. And, really, what could be a better mode of transportation than one that picks up the icy drizzle right off the wet roads and sprays it back into your face, even as you fight for control in the raging gusts?

On our trip to Iceland when I was seven, I wanted adventure, but was pickier about what WAS adventure. A few important things I remember, besides the obvious (hot springs, ponies, and good yogurt), was first finding the chocolate milks were unsatisfying. I remember very clearly Molly telling me to only get THAT brand, because the other one was yucky. I remember going down a water slide and looking at the disco lights and bright lights on the inside as I went down. And the clearest memory that occurred about two million times: Dad handing me soggy gummies.

Also I feel it would just be weird not to include this one: biking, just in general. These memories are kind of negative, because I'd guess that Iceland was my least enjoyable trip. I no longer was interested in if the clouds were shaped like smiley faces.

—Lizzy, remembering the ups and downs of a wet trip

My memories about biking in England were kind of similar to Iceland, except now I was nine. I don't want to list the same things over again, but just the particular stuff. My imagination had gone the story-telling way. Suddenly, things sprouted new possibilities, and old favorites disappeared. My expectations of adventure had increased dramatically, except for the random objects that sprouted a waterfall of imagination. I remember hopping off my Dad's and my bike to feed a pony. Maybe this was the first pre-chewed apple it ever had! Maybe I was saving a tortured starving animal by giving it these spitty remnants.

Maybe there's a wicked witch torturing this horse. I might need to save it! And other random things had the same results. This well is a magic wishing well that will give me a thousand pregnant ponies I can take home in the bike boxes!

However, other things I had no patience for. "Shut up, Dad. No more knock-knock jokes." "How far is it?" "Can we camp yet?"

My imagination was really less random when I was nine than three. However, it still really is kind of the same—and I still have favorite stuffed animals.
–Lizzy, considering how kids' experiences change with age

Given the predilections of our family, it wasn't surprising that we'd plan a non-motorized vacation. Even so, from the earliest planning stages, I'd had a few misgivings about the sanity of the venture. Was I expecting too much of the kids, physically, by planning to cover thirty to fifty miles per day via pedal power? Would even that relatively ambitious mileage be enough to reach an adequate number of Awesome Sights, and to really see a cross-section of Iceland in a mere two weeks? Would we achieve a reasonable balance between time spent pedaling and time spent in non-pedaling Enriching Activities, such as visiting museums, sampling adventuresome foods, gazing at geysers, and diving into inter-cultural conversation? In short, was the idea of biking around Iceland with two seven-year-olds on tag-along bikes completely bats-in-the-treehouse-loony?

In part, my misgivings were based on helpful feedback from friends who told me, in effect, "Bicycling around Iceland with two seven-year-olds on tag-along bikes is bats-in-the-treehouse-loony." My trepidations were also based on a relatively brief perusal of Icelandic weather data.

This is not to say that no one was enthused by the idea of visiting the land of Vikings, fjords, trolls, hot springs, and the Reykjavik Phallus Museum. In fact, most of my acquaintances seemed interested, or even jealous, when I mentioned our destination, especially when I boasted about the astonishing affordability of the airline tickets we'd managed to snag. However, friends and family were flummoxed when we went on to explain that our luggage would include our bikes, our bulging panniers—and nothing else. "What do you plan to do there," one friend asked my, suspicion written all over his face, "besides . . . biking?"

Um . . . well . . .

So, yeah. Here I was, out in the cold rain with nary a Viking ruin, geyser, or waterfall in sight, and my co-pilot was getting peeved. All my guilt and misgivings came rushing back. I was tempted to wail, "You're right! It's NOT fun! I am a fool, a poor deluded fool!" Past experience, however, forewarned me that maternal histrionics would do little to lighten the mood. Instead, I looked around for potential distractions.

"Look! Cows! Let's stop and say hi to them!"

And thus we learned that damp Icelandic cows—who all seem to be of the dairy variety, rather than the more emotionally challenging going-to-get-eaten variety—are a convivial, svelte, politely curious bunch, grass-happy and eager to tell you just how delicious their skyr yogurt is: "Fat free and high in protein! Do try the melon and star fruit flavor!" All the calves are taught perfect English, which is awfully handy for clueless American tourists.

Lizzy cheered up. She counted cows. She told me about which mama cows had twins. Twins!

On we went. Just as the troops were getting restless again, we discovered an experimental forestry plantation. At least, that's what I think it was. The sign said, "Skógræktarfélag Árnesinga," which I took to mean, "nice woodsy place in which some previous traveler in worse straights than you built a rather pathetic lean-to out of sticks." It was an idyllic little sylvan patch in an almost-unforested nation. It felt sheltered, private, ours alone. We never, ever would have stopped at the Skógræktarfélag Árnesinga if we'd been in an automobile . . . or a bus . . . or a Happy Camper van. It was most definitely not on the map.

Not that Off the Map was anything new. From the very beginning of our adventure, we'd been stopping in places that tourists—the kind driving shiny little rental cars or riding in trundling Reykjavik Excursions behemoths—would never, ever bother to examine in miniscule detail. For example, on Day One, we looked at rocks and bones.

That first day of the trip was crystal clear, a blue-sky gift that even the pickiest of travelers could not possibly have complained about. Unfortunately, our flight spat us out at Keklavik airport at 6 a.m., but left our internal body clocks back in Alaska, where it was 10 p.m. the previous evening. Not one of us had slept on the plane—but sleep was no longer an option, now. The only option was biking.

After spending some quality time annoying the airport security folks by fumbling our seven bajillion bicycle parts back together in

> ## TIP ▪ Roadside Entertainment
>
> Bike touring, from an adult perspective, offers a fabulous opportunity to see a new place close-up, at a pace that allows for experiences and observations impossible from a car. This is true for kids, too–but the sights, sounds, smells, and stopping-spots that enchant kids may be entirely different from those that appeal to adults.
>
> In part, this is because kids are less experienced, and thus less jaded. To you, geysers may be novel, whereas cows and hay bales are not. To a kid, all these things might be equally new and fascinating.
>
> Kids also have an unrivaled richness of imagination that can make the mundane magical. We found hours of entertainment in jointly spinning impossible stories about roadside objects. Of particular appeal were tales of altered scale–Gulliver's Travels, of sorts–in which fairies might build whole worlds from leaves, pods, and twigs, or giants might use electrical poles as toothpicks.

an inconvenient lobby, and after desperately searching for—and eventually unearthing—the luggage storage facility, we were all set to hit the road. Except, of course, for the fact that we were blindingly exhausted.

The children biked forty kilometers (twenty-five miles) over the course of four hours. We stopped for snacks. We stopped to look at lava rocks, intricately bubbly little confections that they are. We stopped to look at the tiny wind-dried bones of birds. A seagull skull is a thing of strange and delicate beauty, if you are very, very jet-lagged. At the picturesque campsite in the orderly little fishing village of Grindavik, we sampled a delicious natively greenhouse-grown little melon, into which Lizzy's face slumped as she fell asleep.

And so it continued. On Day Two, after a delightful morning spent both mocking and enjoying the over-hyped Blue Lagoon, we successfully escaped all sign of any other tourists at not one, not two, but THREE fascinatingly arbitrary roadside locations—one for each of Tom's flat tires. The last of these was also our makeshift campsite—last resort of the jet-lagged, headwind-cursed, and puncture-prone—on the gale-swept shores of Kleifarvatn. This deep and ominous lake is draining into a gigantic geological fissure, and is, moreover, frequented by trolls. Or so we heard. We would never, ever have stopped there, had we not been on bikes. I should also mention that the tent almost blew away in the middle of the night.

Day Three was full of new experiences. Such as, for example, coasting uphill. The force of a temperamental (and possibly psychotic) thirty-plus mph Icelandic wind propelled us into

Only seventeen more kilometers to the geyser! Biking in Iceland offered rain and wind, but also some astonishing natural sights. FAMILY PHOTO

Reykjavik—and sometimes perpendicular to Reykjavik, and/or away from Reykjavik. Had we been in a car, we would doubtless not have stopped, dripping, at a suburban grocery store, where we cowered by the unused shopping carts, ate a frightening quantity of chocolate doughnuts, and garnered the quietly amused sympathy of the locals. Nor would we have stopped sixteen or seventeen times at the junctions of the city's extensive and utterly perplexing network of biking/walking paths. In doing so, we had plenty of time to admire the tidy fronts, backs, and sides of hundreds of lovely urban homes. We learned that Reykjavikers push old-fashioned baby carriages. They go running. They plant trees and flowers. They grow cabbages, turnips, and potatoes. And they post lots of signs with little graphics that make it abundantly clear that you need to pick up your dog's crap in a little plastic bag, thank you very much.

Day Four, cloudy with occasional drizzle. But in a city full of bike paths, every fantastic museum is mere minutes away, and parking is oh-so-convenient. Yes, kids, the Vikings came here in the year 871 (plus or minus two). They had fascinating homes with sod roofs, all manner of tools and implements for fishing and farming, and swords to whack each other with. But no bicycles. If they'd had bicycles, maybe they would have spent less time whacking each other with swords. And that thing in the glass case is a sperm whale penis. Now, let's get some falafel sandwiches for lunch. Are you culturally confused yet?

With sunshine on our shoulders, we hit some major tourist hot spots on days five, six, and seven. We visited Þingvellir, where ancient Vikings shouted laws about sheep-stealing at one another. We camped within earshot of Geysir, where hot water breath-stoppingly blasts eighty feet out of the ground—an entirely expected phenomenon that causes dozens of grownups to squeal in surprise. Every. Single. Time. We wandered about in the thunderous spray of Gulfoss, which is humungous. And a waterfall. And beautiful, of course—utterly beautiful.

Many tourists flash along the narrow roads at 90 kph, hitting all these big-name attractions in a single day. But we were on bikes. We were . . . slower.

We were on bikes, and we were also travelling with kids. Thus, we hit some not-so-major tourist attractions: small-town playgrounds; supermarket cafes; an almost infinite supply of adorable Icelandic ponies who obligingly took apple cores from the kids' fingers with gentle, leathery lips; rock piles; interesting and unfathomable signs; home-town hot-tubs in villages almost too small to merit names; and people who wanted to know who the heck we were—and why we were there.

Why was a big question. Sure, there were other bike-touring folks out there—Germans, French, Canadians, Danes, Norwegians, Finns—and there were other tent-campers tucked between the RVs, trailers, and Happy Campers at every campground. But, as we discovered, being a family on bikes made us unique. (A family plus a Tom, that is—but no one ever questioned why there was a stray friend, or perhaps funny uncle or second husband, in our group.) Instead, they wanted to know where we were from (what crazy nation breeds freaks such as these?) and where we were going (how many kilometers can those tiny legs pedal in a day?) and how on earth we had brainwashed our kids into thinking this was fun.

"Mama, this is not fun!"

Well . . . mostly fun. Except for at moments like this. Ok. Time for another stop. Selfoss was an unpromising town, a workaday place about which even the upbeat Lonely Planet guide had nothing in particular to say. But we stopped there for lunch, because . . . Kids. Bikes. Raining. My burden of self-doubt felt heavy again, as I tried to hang little raincoats and little rain pants near the heaters in the pizza joint without hogging more than two tables.

"I hope you don't mind that I took a photo of your bicycles. Where are you from?" The gray-ponytailed guy looked slightly shabby, in a friendly aging hippie Alaskan sort of way, but he was definitely Icelandic. That is, as I soon discovered, he was Icelandic but had lived for some years in the US, where he had married an American of Cherokee descent. They now lived in Stokkseyri. Would we like to visit them? Alas, we weren't going to make it that far that day, but we happily told our newfound friend about our biking adventures. He, in turn, told us about the culture shock his kids suffered when they first moved from California to a small Icelandic fishing village.

It was food for thought. It was a connection, in a country that I perceived as being both friendly and Nordically reserved. And the pizza was pretty darned good, too.

It was still raining when we left Selfoss. The rain gear was immediately soaked again. But a couple of hours later, it hung dripping across half a dozen pegs in the women's locker room at the Eyrerbakki pool. There were no other tourists in the hot tub—or in the locker room. There was, however, a smiling young woman who was curious enough about these odd yet seemingly harmless Americans to engage the kids in conversation. Oh, so they liked the ponies? She herself had forty ponies!

At last I was able to ask all the questions I'd accumulated about the logistics and economics of horse-farming in Iceland (yes, I ruminate about subjects like economics; I can't help myself). Our local interpreter was eager to educate me. Yes, they exported the animals, which were sought-after all over the world. Yes, they got breeding fees for their stallions. Lots of Icelanders simply enjoying riding. And what kind of adventures were we having in her homeland?

Tom and Jay looked a bit perplexed about how long it took for us to emerge from the locker room. They, it seemed, had not engaged in nude chit-chat with any locals.

The young woman was notable for her fantastic English. The previous night, in the non-metropolis of Brautarholt, we'd discovered the Iceland-rare phenomenon of being forced to play we-are-American-idiots charades. The smiling middle-aged man in charge of the pool—and the field next door that served as our official campground, for us and us alone—could not quite work out how to charge us. In fact, he seemed genuinely loath to do so, despite the reasonable posted rates of about six dollars per adult for camping, and about three bucks for all the hot-tubbing we wanted. (Kids were free. Kids were free everywhere.) Likewise, the elderly man trying to recapture his adorable Chocolate Lab puppy didn't speak any English at all. However, with our two kids as puppy-bait, it was easy to help him out—and no one really needed to say anything besides "vinsamlegast" and "takk fyrir."

Come to think of it, who needs English?

That evening—on the same day in which my self-confidence had felt so sodden when the riding was "not fun"—the little town of Eyrarbakki offered a playground, a sandbox with more mysterious bones (just like a REAL archaeologist!), another pool/hot tub combo, and—at last—enough breezy sunshine to nearly dry the laundry, if only it would stop blowing off the line. Yet another Icelandic stranger ambled over and, grinning gently, handed me a bag of clothespins. She looked like a grandma—somebody's grandma, everybody's grandma. I loved her immediately. She told me, in English mostly composed of smiles and nods, that she and her husband were from Heimeay Island. On my map, I found this little swatch of land—perched out in the temperamental ocean off Iceland's south coast. Oh, this was a woman who certainly knew how to hang up laundry in high winds, in the brief respites between rain showers. I accepted the colorful plastic pins gratefully. "Takk fyrir." And everything came together, somehow. Then the trip felt right. Complete.

Sometimes the sun
DID shine during
our 2013 bike tour
in Iceland.
FAMILY PHOTO

Not that our journey was over on the Night of the Clothespins; the very next day we enjoyed two museums, a lava tube, more bubbly geothermal phenomena, and a thoroughly unexpected town-wide carnival. Whoopee, time for the annual Flower Festival in Hveragerði! Moreover, it was gloriously sunny all day, and we enjoyed a helpful yet genteel tailwind. Nonetheless, I'm pretty sure it was not all this photogenic and bikable loveliness that won me over. No, it was in unprepossessing little Eyrarbakki that I finally let go of my guilt, my qualms, and my double-guessing. Biking around Iceland with my husband, my good friend, and my two small children? Yeah, it was a fantastic idea.

What I discovered about biking in Iceland was, essentially, what I already knew about biking in Alaska—and everywhere else. Yes, bicycles are slow, as compared to cars—but only in the same way that home-cooking is slow, as compared to Burger King. Sure, biking can be damp, and cold, and windy, but it can also be blissfully real. A car—with its windows rolled up, the heat blasting, the windshield wipers flapping, and the stereo on—is awfully comfortable, but it's also a cocoon that shuts out the world. It filters out the smell of pony, the faints wafts of sulfur from a cracked and restless earth, and the sharp cries of the gulls.

In contrast, it's impossible to hide on a bike. I'm sure that plenty of people thought we were nuts, but at least we weren't just one more faceless batch of tourists rushing through the Obligatory Sights. On bikes, Molly and Lizzy paid attention to geology, geography, flora, fauna, archaeology, architecture, and infrastructure (Seriously. We're talking major edification!). They also received smiles from old ladies walking dogs, garnered curious stares from kids their own age, and earned spontaneous cheers from construction workers (and who wouldn't appreciate a little attention from a young Viking in a reflective vest?).

In a car, the stereotypical family vacation question is, "Are we there yet?" On a bike, that isn't even really relevant: you're already there. Wherever you happen to be—staring at cows, reading the interpretive plaque by a pair of windmills, catching a glimpse of a nameless waterfall, borrowing a bag of clothespins, or being photographed outside a pizza joint—is part of the fun, and part of the not-fun, and part of everything in between.

No, we didn't see the whole country. But then I haven't seen all of America, either. Yes, it sometimes rained. But Lizzy, at her more whimsical moments, took this in stride, and wove the rain into the stories she was telling me. And we pedaled on.

Takk fyrir, Iceland.

Raising Free-Range Kids

Over the previous couple of years, I'd read a lot of articles about "free range kids." The term—and the movement—was initiated by Lenore Skenazy, the dastardly mother who triggered an uproar when she allowed her nine-year-old to ride the New York City subway alone—and then admitted to it, in print! In truth, Skenazy is a self-proclaimed "safety geek" who nonetheless espouses the notion that kids are capable young individuals who should be allowed and expected, when ready, to do stuff on their own.

Now, my own kids were nine. There are no subways here in Fairbanks, Alaska, but there were other ways for our young poultry to spread their wings. Simply going to the outhouse alone when the thermometer reads forty degrees below zero was a small-scale adventure in self-reliance. The school bus stop was half a mile from our cabin in the woods. At a campground in Denali National Park, I'd put the twins and a young friend in charge of lighting and tending the fire, then wandered off; when I came back forty-five minutes later, they'd not only refrained from setting themselves alight, they'd also baked me a perfect potato.

But I realized that Fairbanks wasn't just a place for Last Frontier Style independence; we could also conjure opportunities for retro nineteen-fifties free-ranging, both figuratively and literally. One day that summer, my friend Laura and I were interrupted in the middle of a carpentry project by a cheerful voice. "Hello! Can you let me know if you see a chicken?"

As a conversational opener, this had promise. We paused our industrious hammering of nails into a nascent shed. The speaker, casually friendly on the edge of the lawn, quickly introduced herself as my friend Laura's new neighbor. She didn't seem unduly worried about her missing bird. "They go wherever they want. They're completely free-range."

The phrase made me involuntarily glance over to where four kids, aged eight and a half through twelve, were busy constructing mysterious items out of scrap lumber. One of my twins was really going to town with the cordless drill. The eldest of the quartet was sweating away with a hand saw.

The fact that the kids were all in view was unusual. The pre-teen had been uncaged for some time. The three younger ones were new to the mean streets—but over the course of the previous two weeks, they had been rampaging around the miniscule metropolis of downtown Fairbanks, undertaking such nefarious pursuits as riding their bikes to a local playground, touring historical buildings, and (horrifying as it may seem) checking out library books.

That's right: my kids, left to their own devices, went and signed themselves up for the Summer Reading Program. According to the Noel Wien Public Library Patron Conduct Policy, " . . . Conduct in the library building or on its premises which may lead to denial of library privileges includes . . . leaving a child under the age of nine unattended in the library . . . " The twins were precisely nine years and five days old, and thus totally kosher, but their scofflaw friend Josie was a mere eight years and seven months. However, as the more diminutive of my kids noted with undisguised jealousy, "Everyone would totally think Josie's nine. Maybe even TEN!" Right. She was practically ready for a fake I.D. Or, like, a fake "Raven About Reading" children's library card. Don't tell the authorities.

But, in truth, free-range parenting is not about making your kids into public nuisances, and it's not about breaking rules; it's about resisting the urge to make too many rules in the first place. It's the antithesis of helicopter parenting. As such, it represents kick-back against what has become the new norm. Skenazy was called "The World's Worst Mother" for letting a nine year-old loose in New York for an hour—but there was no uproar whatsoever when my dad rode the NYC subway to school alone every day when he was just six. There was no uproar when I myself was nine, and my mom hung a house key around my neck on a piece of yarn.

But those were different times, the protest goes. The world is so much more dangerous nowadays. Except that, in fact, it's not. I had to explain to my kids what "mumps" were, when that disease cropped up in one of the aforementioned stories. I've had to define "quarantine," "coal gas," "rationing," and "illegal still," and explain why cars used to have no seat belts and why so many people seemed to be smoking. We've made the world a better, safer, kinder, and more equitable place in a lot of ways that matter. Moreover, crime rates have actually decreased since I was the age my kids are now, when a buddy and I used to rampage around our suburban neighborhood on bikes. The odds have improved. But, barraged with Bad News TV, Americans tend not to believe this.

"Scenarios:" my job title and my research group both include the word, so it looms large in my life. The concept doesn't apply merely to all the ways in which the ice caps might melt or the forests might burn. The future—anyone's future, everyone's future— is a patchwork of possibilities. Some are far more likely than others. Some are desirable, some are benign, and some are so horrific that we want to believe that we can dial their risk down to absolute zero.

Sometimes, we can come pretty darned close. Don't want your kid to end up polio-stricken in an iron lung? Huzzah, there's a handy-dandy vaccine for that! But other choices carry heavier trade-offs. For example, one of the most dangerous things that we Americans allow our kids to do is ride in cars. We can greatly improve the odds by insisting on seat belts and those five-point harnesses that toddlers love so much. But if we wanted to eradicate the risk, we'd have to keep the kids out of vehicles entirely, which . . . yeah. Welcome to reality.

Oddly, what keeps a lot of kids under the whipping blades of helicopter parenting is not the real and tangible hazards of traffic, but the bogeyman of Stranger Danger. I know, I know: the over-hyped news of children-abducted-by-unknown-creeps-or-psychos is scary as hell. It also occurs at an annual rate of approximately 1.25 per million in the US—mathematically insignificant.

The vast majority of the time, we are not helpless in the face of a cruel world, and neither are our kids. It makes sense to talk to children about which potential adult behaviors (even among friends and family . . . no, given the statistics, ESPECIALLY among friends and family) are iffy, untrustworthy, or downright horrendous. Wearing helmets and brightly colored clothing and assiduously following traffic rules reduces the risk associated with riding bikes. It's also important to teach kids to remain alert to the jerks who are too busy texting to know how to drive.

The tradeoffs for doing all of the above are . . . Being dorky? Having helmet-hair? I'm cool with that. But some risk still exists. The only way to reduce kids-on-bikes injuries to zero is to never let kids bike at all. This is not a trade-off I'm willing to consider. Nor am I willing to tell children to never speak to anyone they haven't met before.

The optimal number of kids for free-ranging expeditions, in my opinion, is between two and four. One kid alone is vulnerable, particularly if something goes wrong or they get hurt. Groups of more than four are unwieldy and tend to fall apart organizationally, leading to stragglers and/or poor group choices.

Ultimately, the woman with the missing chicken reported that all her free-rangers were accounted for. Then she invited the human free-rangers to come and visit. Apparently her birds like hugs. "And at night, they just kind of pick a tree, and roost there."

I couldn't stop myself from picturing four children cozily roosting in some kind of homemade treehouse. They'd love that. What free-ranger wouldn't?

On Their Own: Setting Kids Loose

I said goodbye to the two of them at the roundabout. They pedaled away from me, pigtails poking from beneath helmets, little twenty-inch tires churning. They didn't look back.

As I ran up the hill to West Ridge, the road's shoulder looked narrower than I remembered, and the slope seemed steeper and longer. Would they have to walk their bikes, when it was time for them to find me? What about the two busy roads they needed to cross, both coming and going? Would they correctly calculate what lunches they could purchase with the money I'd provided? Did they remember the combination to the bike lock? How about the location of my new office? What if . . .

No. Stop. I opened the glass doors to the university building full of offices and lab space. I jogged up two flights of stairs and around the corner to an office decorated with a medley of artwork from grades K-3. I fired up my computer. The kids would buy their sandwiches at the café in Gulliver's Books, I told myself. They would peruse a few used paperbacks. They might count up their change and buy a caramel or two from the alluring box by the cash register. And then, in two hours' time, they'd bike up the hill. My little free-rangers would be just fine.

Unaccompanied Kids' Bike Ride

Location ▪ From the University of Alaska to a nearby café and bookstore, West Fairbanks.

Distance and duration ▪ About 4 miles round trip.

Locomotion ▪ Kids' bikes with 7 gears and 20 inch wheels.

Terrain ▪ Somewhat hilly. Road shoulders, bike paths, and sidewalks.

Weather ▪ Warm and sunny, about 70°F.

Accommodations ▪ Urban and semi-urban amenities, with reliable traffic lights.

Bikes provide independence to young explorers ready to start having their own small adventures—a mile from home, in Fairbanks, Alaska.
FAMILY PHOTO

Up in my office, I waded through the slurry of emails swamping my inbox. I battled a spreadsheet into submission. I quickly rummaged for my lunch in the break-room fridge, which was adorned with a discomfiting laminated note reminding everyone to refrain from storing scientific experiments therein. What were the kids eating down at Gulliver's? They loved taking command of the little wipe-off cards that allowed them to write what kinds of bread and fillings they preferred. Toasted or not toasted? Provolone or Cheddar? With the shredded carrot? The spinach? Oh, the thrill of it! They could take ten minutes to carefully plan a sandwich.

Being in control turns the humdrum into an adventure. This piece of kid-psychology isn't new-fangled. Classic novels I'd passed on to my children over the past couple of years—books by Elizabeth Enright and Arthur Ransome—feature buccaneers as young as six joining older siblings in adult-free urban exploration, rural camping, and sailing. It warmed my heart to see my third-grader burying her nose in a four-hundred-page moldy-looking volume that once belonged to my mother. That the story in those pages involved bold and unapologetic free-range girls pretending to be Amazon pirates—well, that was pure perfection.

Math. Spreadsheets. I glanced at the clock. What if someone saw the twins out there, and didn't share my views on parenting? It didn't help that my nine-year-olds looked younger than their years. One of them was barely the size of the average first grader. What if someone thought . . . No. I glanced resolutely at my emails again: Climate change scenarios planning . . . .

One thirty. They'd be leaving the bookstore now—if they remembered what we'd agreed, and if they remembered to look at their watches. Two traffic lights. One roundabout. And those two awkward three-way intersections protected only by stop signs. But they knew enough to make the right choices.

The twins' ninth birthday party had occurred on a gloriously sunny day at a sprawling public park. I'd interrupted the young revelers in their primary activity (spraying one another with muddy water from the drainage ditch that masquerades as a stream) to send them off on a somewhat quirky scavenger hunt. Not only had this provided the lingering adults with the chance to create a grownup mini-party, it also had given the kids a chance to accost totally unknown park-goers with odd requests. "Can you please tell me who was President when you were nine?" Go learn some history, children. Also, please talk to strangers.

It was only a mile or so from the bookstore to my office, but it was all uphill. It would take them a while on those six-geared bikes. They would press the buttons and wait for the Walking Person. They would look both ways, cautious for the type of drivers who think that "right turn on red" is one of the Ten Commandments. Spreadsheets. Back to my spreadsheets. They would come back.

Ping! A message. Quickly, I clicked.

"As I finished crossing the street on today's expedition to Pad Thai, I was accosted by . . . "

Yeah. By my children.

Connotations for the word "accosted" notwithstanding, this was not a message from Social Services. Nor was it a message from the State Troopers, Fairbanks Memorial Hospital, or the FBI. No, via the sweet serendipity of small-town life, the writer was my friend Paul, father of the twins' free-ranging, tool-using, library-rule-flouting co-conspirators.

" . . . What a pleasure it was to see those strong, independent, skillfully biking young women."

Young women! Ha. On one hand, it seemed like a stretch to describe my freckled, scabby-kneed pipsqueaks in such a manner. On the other hand . . . growing up is incremental. That's the whole point, isn't it? A grin spread across my face.

And then, impeccably timed, I heard an ebullient chirrup at my elbow.

"Hi Mom! We're here!"

Cluck. Cluck. Good little chicks.

Canines as Inspiration

"Well, the dogs need a walk, anyhow."

It was February. It was cold—because February. It was getting dark, because ditto. There was more unbroken snow on the trails than I really wanted to deal with. I knew I'd have to reduce the pressure in the wide tires of my fat-bike down to almost nothing in order to avoid sinking, wallowing, and creating hopeless ruts. It really wasn't a great day for a ride. But I knew I needed to get in some training for the White Mountains 100, if I was going to make it around that giant loop in one piece the following month. I knew I'd be happier if I spent some time outside. I knew the kids would be happier if they went with me. And . . . the dogs needed a walk. In the teetering scale of my mid-winter decision-making, the dogs are so often what tip things in the right direction.

"Okay," Molly turned to Lizzy. "You want to skijor, or Mom-jor?"

Here's some translation for anyone who hasn't spent at least a few winters in the far north: Skijoring is the delightful and surprisingly adrenaline-boosting sport of Nordic skiing in a hip harness, with one or more sled dogs pulling you along. Mom-joring, a less familiar term, refers to the same thing while attached to the frame of my snow bike.

> Dogs are bouncy, excitable creatures. Often, they can get you moving, or push you off the fence of whether to go or not to.
>
> Our dogs turn into hyperactive maniacs if they stay inside, or outside too long without moving. I, too, usually feel better after going outside and moving with them.
>
> *–Lizzy, on the merits of canines*

I should pause here to say a word or two about sled dogs. They are loveable. They are delightful. They are really, really furry. And wow, do they love to pull stuff.

Although our dogs have always blatantly been pets rather than working animals, they have provided us with a fair amount of labor, especially when the kids were very small. Over the years, we've used them to pull heavyweight plastic gear sleds (pulks); a baby-hauling sled with plastic roll-bars, a hand-sewn cover, and bolted-in car seats; and a child-sized mushing sled.

At first, we were a bit nervous about allowing our infants to be pulled by high-energy canines, but the dogs were trained to heel rather than lead, and they trotted along patiently with their load. We occasionally had to untangle the sled from shrubbery, or flip it back to an upright position when a rut, corner, or bank caused it to roll. Amazingly, the babies didn't even wake up when this happened.

Every year, I see anxious posts online about the Iditarod from Outsiders (the term Alaskans use for non-Alaskans, sometimes with the inflection that a wizard might use when saying "muggles").

> I remember getting my very first skis. I was only two. The skis were fifty centimeters long. We couldn't find boots that were small enough to fit our feet, so we wore big ones with many layers of socks. When we first started out, we didn't use poles. I think it's better to learn without poles, so kids learn to balance.
> —Molly, on how to introduce toddlers to skis

These posts are mostly from well-meaning animal lovers and animal rights activists who are concerned about the welfare of dogs running a thousand miles and pulling sleds through the frigid Alaskan wilderness. And I get it: it sounds pretty extreme. But you only have to meet a handful of sled dogs to hear their eloquent (albeit limited) side of the story. It sounds something like this:

"Go? Go? Go? Can we go now? Please please please please please? Yes? Yes! Yes yes yes yes yes! Run! Pull, pull, pull, run! Yay!" With a few extremely rare and sad exceptions, regarded with enormous outrage by all Alaskans, mushing dogs are not being forced, coerced, or abused. They just really like to go running and pulling. A lot.

Of course, this is true of most canines, to a greater or lesser degree. Even the most primped and highly bred lapdog secretly wants to let loose her inner feral wolf and run through the forest sniffing moose poop. Indeed, this is what goes through my mind every time I see a really pampered dog.

I wasn't raised to think of pets as integral members of the American family. I can remember when I was first learning to read, I marched up to my mother with one of my favorite picture books, A Hole is to Dig. "You've been reading this wrong," I accused, pointing to the offending page. I'd been led to believe the words said 'A dog is to play with.' My mother did not apologize for her blatant falsification. "Well, 'A dog is to kiss' is disgusting," she said.

Neither of my parents likes dogs much, and as a small child I was petrified of all dogs, large and small. In part, I was channeling my parents' feelings, but I also didn't know any nice canines. There was one particularly vicious little creature that got loose and took a bite out of Mom's leg. The kids up the street had two dogs, but both of them seemed to be brain-damaged. The small dog skittered around spasmodically on the linoleum, and the big dog barked and growled on a heavy chain, as if it might eat any child who strayed too close. There were also some large, menacing strays that skulked around the colonial-era cemetery up the street. It wasn't until we moved to a different neighborhood, when I was almost ten, that I met some stereotypically benevolent Golden Retrievers and a charming three-legged mutt named Bacchus who had apparently been abandoned in a bar.

Our own dogs—the ones I acquired as an adult, in Alaska—have all had equally inglorious histories and sweet dispositions. All of them have been sled dogs in the loosest sense, meaning they have thick coats that allow them to live outside year-long, though their parentage is iffy, mixed, and mysterious.

Togiak was an accident puppy in a mushing yard. She was passed on to a teenage musher, a friend of Jay's sister, but flunked out even there as a weakling. Jay adopted her in 1999, when she was a submissive, shoe-chewing two-year-old. It turns out Togiak wasn't really a wimp. She just had a bit of a thyroid problem. Lots of years and approximately six thousand Soloxine tablets later, she finally called it quits at the age of eighteen. Forty-five-pound dogs don't live that long, but ours did.

Polar was also born to mush. There was never anything wrong with him physically. He was a lean, leggy athlete, and he could pull a sled like nobody's business. However, to the dismay of his original owners, he much preferred chasing a tennis ball to winning a race.

The entire concept of competition was lost on him. But he was always pathetically eager to please, and happy to help haul our gear sled, or our baby-hauling sled, or even (in his ripe old age) the kids' miniature mushing sled. Polar lived to sixteen, and I'm pretty sure he just really loved being himself.

Then there were Remus and Shiloh. Remus came from the shelter as a rail-thin young adult of entirely mysterious origins. When the kids were nine, he was twelve, but thought he was twelve months. He had a nice thick coat that got him through Fairbanks winters

Canines provide boundless inspiration for playing outside. FAMILY PHOTO

with ease, he was tough as they come and oh-so-enthusiastic, but he was built like a wombat. His short legs churned through the snow and his tongue hung several miles out of his mouth. In his prime, a fifty-mile day was nothing to Remus, although you had to wait for him on the downhills. Ultimately, he also made it to his sixteenth winter, and even in his last months he was eager to run, and utterly unconcerned about his own mortality. Dogs are great that way.

Shiloh, meanwhile, was only two when we got him, another pound dog, rescued near starving from a dump. He's a mellow gangly, floppy-eared boy, congenitally allergic to seemingly everything. We dose him with anti-itch medication and antihistamines, but he still sneezes and snorts and whuffles. He doesn't seem to mind in the least. He's not self-conscious about his mucus. Dogs are great that way, too.

Later, after losing Remus, we acquired Eddie. He's another mushing dog whose owner wanted to find him a good new home, due to a slightly injured foot. He runs just fine, but is not a thousand-miler. He doesn't seem to mind. Dogs are great that way, too.

In many ways, dogs are better suited for life in Alaska even than humans. I can't locate half a cookie in a pile of rotting leaves by smell alone. I can't catch shrews with my bare hands, sleep naked in a pile of straw at forty below, run sixty miles in a day, or find my way home through the forest on a moonless January night. I also have trouble providing companionship, comfort, and hours-long hugs to those I love without excessive analysis, judgment, conversation, and expectations. The specific greatness of dogs is one of the things that makes them such excellent companions.

The kids were experts, by age nine, at getting their warm gear and their ski boots on, grabbing their skis, harnessing up Shiloh, setting Remus free from his chain, finding the appropriate ropes and clips and webbing, hooking up humans, dog, and bike—and doing it all in huge mittens. It didn't take long before we were moving along the trail—not at rocket-speed, but at a decent clip. For me, it was resistance training. For the dogs, it was sheer joy. And joy, of course, is catching.

Dogs are good at being dogs. On a good day, I am semi-adequate at being a human. But when we meet in the middle, everything works out just fine.

Age 10 and Up: Hey, Wait for the Grownups . . .

Kids Taking the Lead

Big kids are fantastic trip companions. They are strong enough, both mentally and physically, to keep up with the adults. They don't get sore and arthritic and creaky. They play games on the trail, but they don't insist on always playing games when the older, creakier people are so, so done with games. They see the things that adults are too jaded to see, and they laugh more often than we do. They can now carry an appropriate amount of the gear, help keep track of the dogs, and take on a lot of the camp chores on overnight trips. The twins by now are getting pretty good with axes and saws, and they pride themselves on their excellent campfire-starting abilities—even after heavy rain, and even without the benefit of paper or other "cheats."

Sometimes older kids disappear in packs, gangly and self-assured. Make sure that if they are unsupervised, they have everything with them that an adult

I'm sure that everyone has had someone somewhere saying, "Kids these days, always on the computer!" Motivating to go on trips is good, but how do you motivate kids to go outside? Forcing kids to go outside never works. Telling kids to get off the computer makes them defensive, and even less likely to stop, even if they were just watching a video that they've watched eight million times already. Giving the kid the responsibility of a dog is good, because dogs need exercise and love getting it. Kids love dogs. I've had my friends beg me to take the leash. Trust me.

Also, outdoor projects are great. This summer, Molly, Laurel (a friend), and I cut length after length of dead wood from black spruces with hand saws. We didn't notch them, but stacked them on top of each other, and chinked the gaps with lots of moss. The result: we had a log cabin in our woods with two bunks, two rooms, and we woke early in the morning and spent seven entire days outside.
—*Lizzy, reflecting on motivation for older kids*

would have (food, water, rain gear, layers of warm clothing) and that they know everything an adult would need to know (moose safety, bear safety, trail etiquette, Not Getting Lost). Then pick a meet-up point. It's fun watching them go.

The ten-year-olds are in the lead as we crest a ridgeline on the Chena Dome Trail. FAMILY PHOTO

The Same Trip is Different Each Year

The kids have hiked to Tolovana under their own power every year since they were five. As noted, that pre-kindergarten trip was epic—joyful and ultimately triumphant, but a slog at the limits of childish endurance. Only one of the kids' friends came along then; the rest of the parents were not that crazy.

Since then, others have joined us. The twins are picky about who they invite, reserving the honor of the Tolovana tradition for only their closest and most stalwart friends. By my tally, ten different kids have made the trip, some many times over. The year they were eleven, the twins hiked with four friends. They carried their own packs, managed their own snacks, water, and layering systems, and played their own trail games. The group spread out along the trail, adults and kids, into friendly similarly-paced gaggles. I ended up chatting with Emma's dad Andrew. For the first time in eleven years, I hiked ten miles with an adult.

We were not exactly being left in the dust. Some of the kids were ahead of us, and some were behind us. In our defense, our packs were heavier than what the kids were toting, even taking body

Tolovana Hot Springs

Location ▪ Private leased property, 2.5 hour drive northwest of Fairbanks.

Distance and duration ▪ 20 miles round trip, with two days of hiking and a rest day in between (two overnights at the hot springs).

Locomotion ▪ Hiking, with kids carrying reasonable shares of the gear.

Terrain ▪ Hilly, with a clear and well-marked trail, but 2-3 miles of swampy lowlands.

Weather ▪ Clear and sunny fall weather, around 50°F.

Accommodations ▪ Comfortable rental cabins with bunks, wood stoves, propane stoves, and solar/LED lighting. Rustic natural hot tubs.

weight into account. My sense of any profound difference from earlier trips was not an issue of speed but of neediness. As I talked with a grownup about Grownup Things such as politics and the PTA, I was aware of all the things I wasn't doing that I had done on these hikes before.

I wasn't handing out gummy bears. I wasn't singing. I wasn't consoling anyone who was upset about being muddy or tired or getting the wrong color gummy bear. I wasn't coaching anyone in how to poop in the woods.

When we arrived at the hot springs, the girls quickly gathered to claim whatever they deemed the best of the three hot tubs as theirs, at least temporarily. Gone were the days when I'd need to be hot tub supervisor in a seething mass of kids, subjected to being decorated with algae and climbed upon. I had . . . personal space!

I loved it, but I also felt a stab of nostalgia. Sometimes I like singing on the trail. Sometimes I like playing twenty questions and I Spy. And those algae outfits I was made to wear were honestly pretty cool.

On my first Tolovana trip, it seemed like the trail was going on forever. Each time we saw a milepost, we got really happy. At about mile five, at the top of a mountain, there is an empty water tank that has a doorway cut out of it so it can be used as an emergency shelter. On the inside, the plastic walls have written on them the words: HELLO YELLOW KEEP IT MELLOW. We bounced up and down shouting these words over and over again.

Every year now, we stop there, and it has gained the name "The Marshmallow" for the way it looks. This year's trip, as I passed each corner, I would tell Emma what would come around the corner: "Oh, there's a big puddle around this corner, Emma." And sure enough, there's the big puddle, just like I said.

I know that trail really well. Maybe because I've done it nine times. Just maybe.

—Molly, on the joys of revisiting favorite trails

My Packraft is Full of Hail

"Are you okay up there, Molly? Are you warm enough?

"Um . . . sort of? There's . . . kind of a lot of hail in the boat." This was supposed to be spring.

Everyone knows that spring float trips are lazy. You bob along in the sunshine, letting the flow of the river do the work, paddling in a leisurely and sporadic manner in order to stay in the fastest-moving portion of the river as it bends and winds across an idyllic landscape of gravel bars and dense woodland. The sun, of course is shining.

Except when someone forgets to give the sun the memo.

"If you paddle really hard, you'll be warmer, maybe? Are your hands warm enough?"

"Um, yeah, I'm okay."

Sitting in front of me in our two-person craft, Molly was a bundled mass of fleece, neoprene, coated nylon, and stoicism. I couldn't see what conditions looked like around her lap and feet, but I could guess, based on

Beaver Creek to the Summit Trail

Location ■ White Mountains north of Fairbanks, starting at Nome Creek trailhead off the Steese Highway, and finishing at mile 28 of the Eliot Highway.

Distance and duration ■ Two days of floating (~30 miles) and two days of hiking (~20 miles).

Locomotion ■ Pack-rafting in double boats, each with one child and one adult, followed by hiking, with kids and adults all carrying gear.

Terrain ■ Fairly flat water, although shallow in places. Hiking hilly and brushy, with trail difficult to follow in some places.

Weather ■ Hail and rain, around 30-40°F on the water, but later hot and sunny during the hike.

Accommodations ■ Tent camping, with a rest stop at a BLM cabin (Borealis) and a campsite next to a shelter cabin on the Summit Trail. Treated creek water for drinking. Open campfires.

my own. Slithering piles of hail bounced through the folds of my rain gear. My toes were decidedly damp. Not the refreshing kind of damp—the immersed-in-icewater kind of damp. I plied my paddle, and felt the frigid water of Beaver Creek trickle down my wrists on every stroke.

This was supposed to be spring.

A few feet away from us, I could see Lizzy in the front of Jay's boat. Mummified in her own layers of sweaters and raingear, wedged in front of him in the packraft, and clutching her double-ended paddle, it was hard for her to move at all, let alone paddle effectively, but she seemed to be doing her best. She had pulled

> "Steer away from the rocks!" Dad's voice was overly cheerful, as Mom and Molly in the pack raft a few feet away started planning a hail-ball fight between the boats.
>
> "I can't!"
>
> "Why can't you?"
>
> I turned my head toward where Dad would be. My neck-gaiter and hat were pulled over my entire face. "The hail kept going into my eyes! You have to do the steering now."
>
> Dad started grumbling about how this wasn't fair. Just because he didn't bring enough face coverage doesn't mean he can whine.
>
> *–Lizzy, on finding humor in a hailstorm*

her hood and hat down to her eyebrows and her fleece neck-gaiter up over her nose. All I could see were her eyeballs—but they were plenty eloquent. We were not having fun.

But, darn it, this was spring!

Granted, the spring season in Fairbanks is not precisely what other people might think of as "spring" elsewhere. For one thing, the first three quarters of it—all of April and the first half of May—involve not so much bright little flowers as vast piles of slush. But late May is spring for real. By late May, all the spring-y things show up in a frantic rush. Buds! Leaves! Happy little singing migratory birdies

Hail and sleet in the White Mountains made for challenging conditions in the double pack-raft.
Family Photo

whose species I ought to be able to identify, but definitely can't! Late May is glorious.

Except when it isn't.

We planned our float trip carefully, picking the final weekend of the month, when school had just ended for the year and the rivers should still be relatively full from the snow-melt, but not actually snowy. We gathered a whole passel of friends with a motley flotilla of crafts: our two double pack rafts, four single pack rafts, and our good friends Trusten and Robin, an indomitable father-and-teen-daughter duo in an extraordinarily iffy canoe.

The owners of this last vessel planned to stash it in the shrubbery at the end of the float and retrieve it the following winter by snowmachine. This bold plan, I must point out, worked out precisely as planned. Other aspects of the trip—not so much.

"How much further are we going today?" Molly inquired, with the careful nonchalance of someone who is definitely not complaining.

"Oh, we just need to cover a few more miles," I told her, with some false cheerfulness, even though I knew she, having turned eleven that week, was probably too old to believe my tone.

An unexpected summer hailstorm shed light-beams and ice flecks on the waters of Beaver Creek FAMILY PHOTO

I heard a similar question being asked in the other double pack raft, with somewhat less studied casualness. I heard the response, and the terse response to the response. Lizzy was definitely not buying Jay's assertion that hail is fun. But there wasn't much choice. We really did need to cover a few more miles.

We'd planned two days of floating and two days of hiking. Our itinerary was only mildly ambitious. In the past, Jay and others had managed the whole jaunt—the float down Beaver Creek from the Nome Creek put-in off the Steese Highway to Borealis Cabin and the 19-mile hike out to the main White Mountains trailhead at mile 28 of the Eliot Highway—in just two days. (Jay asserted that this had been lots of fun; Beth agreed that it had been lots of fun, but also something of a death march). But this was also our very first pack raft trip with the double boats with the kids.

As a mixture of water and hailstones sloshed around my feet, I glanced with envy at the four people—Beth, Constantine, Tom, and Gregg— in single pack rafts. It wasn't so much that those little boats, like a colorful rubber-duck flotilla, looked slightly more maneuverable than mine, but that they had spray-skirts. The hail bounced off them comically. I imagined dry feet.

At least I was wearing neoprene socks. And the kids were in their full-on mud-boots—an item of apparel that my British mother would call Wellingtons. Wellingtons are a springtime necessity in Fairbanks. "Are your toes warm, Molly?"

"Um . . . yeah, they're okay."

So, yeah, we weren't excellent, or spiffy, or elated. We were . . . okay.

Over in Jay's boat, Lizzy seemed to have found herself a groove, too. She was relating to her boat-mate all the plot details, character details, and nuances of the book series she was immersed in at the time—the Warriors novels. Given that the collection involves over forty weighty volumes, I figured that the rest of the float should zoom by. Those two were also . . . okay.

The thing about "okay" is that it averages out, over the course of an adventure. At that moment in time, the trip was not a remarkable success. But catalogued across all four days, the summary went as follows:

On the first day of the float, it hailed—but the sun peeked out in the evening, the dry driftwood was copious, and the kids got to set fire to things all by themselves. We dried out all our gear on a welcoming gravel bar, giggled around the crackling fire, and roasted marshmallows. Marshmallows!

On the second day of the float, it also hailed. But we got a fire going in the Borealis Cabin and thawed our hands and our spirits before packing up the boats and starting the uphill slog. And our campsite was dry, and in an old burn. More fire! More marshmallows! And enough stick-like dead trees for Lizzy to build a fascinating teepee-style playhouse.

On day three, the first full day of the hike, it was unpleasantly hot and muggy—but we had to keep long pants on, because the dense brush that had overgrown much of the trail tore at our shins.

(For Lizzy, the shortest member of the group, the brush tore at much more than her shins). But our campsite was by the trail shelter, and there were comforts like an outhouse and folding chairs. And, of course, more fire—and an even cooler kid-constructed playhouse.

On the last day, the brush receded to a polite distance. The sun beamed down from clear skies. Ten miles seemed like nothing at all. Hail? The hail was no biggie. The trip was perfect.

Perfect trips are all the more perfect for their imperfections.

Getting snacks for trips can be fun. Packing for trips is one of the only times that I'm ever allowed to walk around the store dumping whatever sugary treat I want into our cart. By age eleven, we could pack our snack-bags without any help. I usually pack a good balance of sweet and salty snacks, such as gummies, Goldfish, chocolate, a sandwich, and dried fruit. A good snack bag will keep me happy throughout the day.
–Molly, advocating for autonomous selection of motivational junk food

But How Do You Deal with . . . Rain

Getting wet is not a big deal, if you have a way to get dry again. If you're merely on a day hike with kids, this may be as simple as bringing a change of clothes to put on them when they are (for sure!) done playing in mud puddles. On longer adventures and further afield, quick-dry clothing is enormously helpful.

I've mentioned the downsides of cotton. Jeans, t-shirts, and sweatpants are all great at home, but they are heavy, bulky, worse than useless when wet, and incredibly slow to dry. You already know this, based on their behavior in your dryer.

Outdoor retailers sell lots of different quick-dry fabrics, but any lightweight nylon shirt and pants will dry fast. If wool or fleece items get soaked, be sure to wring them out thoroughly before hanging them up near a wood stove, in the top of your tent, or even flapping off the back of your bike for some quick wind-drying action.

But what if you're biking . . . and it's raining at the time?

One morning some years ago, my friend Paul (who may or may not have been feeling a trace grouchy about the prevailing meteorological conditions) asked me for advice on how to be happy in the rain. He didn't specify, but I had my suspicions that he was referring to a very special subset of precipitational joy: biking in the rain.

Upon receipt of his missive, I was "lucky" enough to spend the following hour in up-close and specific study of this very subject, during which time I mentally threw together a list of Super Helpful Advice.

1) Thermoregulation

This is first because it's the most important thing. Really. Being too cold is miserable. Being a hot sack of homo-sapiens-raingear-sweat is also less than desirable. Being soaking wet, on the other hand, doesn't necessarily suck. Case in point: you do occasionally shower, right? Right?

2) Fenders

See photographic evidence. Being wet is okay, so long as the wetness is the dewy sky-sprinkling of pure and joyous rain-prisms. The gritty road-poop of wheel-spun crud is less splendid, unless you're an insanely cheerful five-year-old, specially bred for that purpose.

3) Clothes that are not utterly gross when wet (see #1)

If it's too hot to pedal in full raingear, or any raingear at all, you should be wearing something minimalist that approximates swimwear: say, Teva sandals, a nylon tank top and lightweight nylon shorts with a liner. Biking across town in a bathing suit is also an

Bike fenders would have been a good idea on a wet day on the unpaved Denali Park Road. FAMILY PHOTO

acceptable strategy, and has been successfully road-tested by one of my family members. I'm not divulging which one, but I trust your powers of imagination.

4) Change of clothes for when you get there

I'm making the bold assumption that "there" is somewhere that does not appreciate drippy, gritty, slightly steaming people. A shower at your destination is a nice bonus, but if not, you too can be the person sponging off your children with paper towels in a public restroom.

5) Raingear

Yeah, this is kind of far down the list. Most people think of this first, not fifth. However, the truth is that raingear is hot and awkward and inevitably a bit leaky, in an up-the-sleeves-and-down-the-neck kind of way. It's what you use when it's too cold to bike in your swimwear, and too hot to be snowing (which is a different essay; ask again in September). It's worth investing in a rain jacket that is lightweight, at least a bit breathable (see #1), fully waterproof, and long enough to cover your butt in the back (see #2). As for rain pants, just get the bombproof cheap kind that make you look like some kind of obsessive fisherman. Then when they get torn or covered in chain oil, you'll just look like a more authentic obsessive fisherman. When they were little, my kids even biked in their colorful little rubber boots, with their home-sewed rain pants pulled down over the tops. It won't look cute when you do it.

6) Umbrellas

If you are not biking, not hiking, and in fact not moving too much or using your hands in any way, and if you are located somewhere with no wind, no trees, and no other people around (or, at least, only people who like being repeatedly poked in the eye), then an umbrella might be extremely handy. Or so I hear. I do not own an umbrella.

So there you have it: Rainy Day Happiness!

Of course, some of you may have noticed that this list is missing a crucial element, which we should probably call "Being crazy." When biking in the rain, it is crucial to persuade yourself, your companions, your children, and all the people passing you in weatherproof vehicles, that you are having a seriously splendid time.

Because, well, obviously.

Type Two Fun: The Joy of Recollection

Molly's sixth grade teacher asked his students to write an essay about the hardest thing they'd ever done, physically. She and her friend Emma both picked the same topic: one of our family hikes. The words "disaster" and "doom" featured heavily in both accounts.

I wasn't sure whether to be wryly amused, or horrified. What would Mr. Harper think of our parenting skills? Our wilderness skills? Our judgement? On the other hand, being blown off Chena Dome in a raging gale of sideways sleet and chilly, plodding despair does make for a riveting tale.

Over the past eleven years, Jay and I have tried hard to introduce our twin daughters to all that is joyful, relaxing, invigorating, and beautiful about the Great Outdoors. However, along the way, inevitably, we've also introduced them to the concept of Type Two Fun.

"Type Two Fun" is a phrase that I first heard bandied about

Chena Dome Trail Loop

Location ▪ Chena River Recreation Area, east of Fairbanks.

Distance and duration ▪ ~30 miles, three days and two nights, as planned. Actual time and distance ended up being similar.

Locomotion ▪ Hiking, with kids carrying their share of the gear.

Terrain ▪ Very hilly, although never technical; trail well marked, but extremely hard to follow above tree line in rain/fog.

Weather ▪ Sun on first day, then increasing fog, wind, and rain, increasing to very high winds above tree line.

Accommodations ▪ Parking area at trailhead. Tent camping only. Bailed out by bushwhacking down to the Upper Angel Creek Cabin, which was unoccupied. Finished the hike by hiking out on the Angel Creek Trail.

TOP The weather and the views were beautiful on the first day of a three-day trip on Chena Dome Trail.

BOTTOM On our second day on the trail, ominous weather rolled over the Chena Dome ridgeline. FAMILY PHOTOS

"Would you like to go on a trip with your friend?" That was what my dad asked before it all started. Lizzy, Emma and I were definitely not expecting what happened next . . .

It was a beautiful day and the trail looked so promising. We went up, up, and up some more until my legs felt like jelly. Then to my relief my mom told us we could find a place to camp.

The next day we started the hard part. The first thing we did was climb to the top or the ridge. Halfway up the hill we saw that something was wrong. We couldn't even see the top of the mountain because it was so foggy. My heavy backpack and I could lean into the wind without falling over. To make it all worse, it was raining, the droplets hitting our faces with the force of a bullet.

Eventually the wind and rain were so strong that we had to do something about it, so our dad led us down through the woods into the valley. Finally we reached the trail, and trudged along to the Upper Angel Creek Cabin. After lighting a fire and changing our clothes, we all felt a lot better. Mom took our clothes outside to wring them out, they were that wet!

The next morning we had to hike back out to our car nine miles on the trail. Surprisingly, the nine miles felt like nine yards after what we'd done the day before.

A tip for hikers, next time you go on a trip, check the weather first.

–Molly, reflecting on a classic "type two fun" experience

among my hiking buddies in college. I don't know whether we made it up, or gleaned it from some invisible collective of outdoor lore. Either way, its definition is relatively simple: Type Two Fun is how one describes any adventure that makes a terrific story after the fact—despite not being actually fun at all, in the moment.

Although a few of my most turbo-charged and mentally questionable friends might disagree, most people don't set out to create

High winds and icy rain made for a less than stellar bushwhack down to safety, off the Chena Done Trail—but provided great material for a school essay. FAMILY PHOTO

Type Two Fun. Reasonable people seek only Type One Fun, otherwise known as, well . . . actual fun. In our imaginings, time outdoors involves sunny picnics on mountaintops, glorious cloud-free vistas, stellar wildlife viewing (at a scenic yet comfortably safe distance), and a marked lack of punctured bike tires, blisters, hail, and exploding diapers.

In real life, results may vary.

Every excursion and adventure described in this book was intended to generate Type One Fun. Backcountry ski trips to cozy cabins with crackling fires! Hikes over glorious ridgetops to natural hot springs! Bike rides along well-maintained trails under sunny skies! We genuinely love this stuff, and we want you to have a blast, too. Indeed, when we provide advice about what to wear, what to pack, and what to avoid, it's almost all aimed at helping to keep fun safely in the Type One zone.

Well-planned adventures vastly reduce the chances of scrapes, sprains, chills, misery, and disaster. Some risks are not to be messed with, especially if you live at a latitude famous for hypothermia, frostbite, and bears. Serious backcountry knowledge is necessary to avoid more serious potential dangers. Nevertheless, into every life of adventure, some Type Two Fun will descend. You will come out of it none the worse for wear. And it will make for a great sixth-grade essay.

Adding More Kids to the Group

Taking along other people's kids on outdoor adventures is both a wonderful idea and a terrible one. Over the years, we have taken unrelated little people ranging in ages from four to twelve on adventures from the tame (an hour-long bike ride, a short hike, a 5K race) to the less tame (a three-day backcountry backpacking trip).

On the plus side, kids love each other's company. Especially if you have just one of your own, bringing a friend will make everyone

This experienced crew of backpackers have all hiked the ten-mile trail to Tolovana Hot Springs many times. FAMILY PHOTO

Getting older kids to motivate is slightly harder than younger ones. It is best to take kids on hikes when they're young, so then the exercise is built into their life from a young age. For me, trips are way more motivating when I have a friend along, so I have someone to talk to. It distracts me, especially when I'm tired, that I have to place one foot in front of the other. Also, figure out what your kid really wants. Will they be happier going to a cabin, or camping in a tent? Having a trip geared to them will make it so that they are more likely to be happy and will be more likely to want to go on a trip next time.

–Lizzy, on involving kids in trip planning

much, much happier. Kids also hold onto their pride in front of their friends—and that means less whining. Then there's the joy of introducing more kids to the things you love. I've taught other people's children to ride a bike, to set up a tent, to light a fire, and (as noted) to poop in the woods. The more the merrier!

And yeah, there are a few downsides. How much extra gear can you carry? How much extra responsibility are you willing to shoulder? How well do you know this family? This kid? Will you end up in an existential hell, or a lawsuit, or both? I've been in charge of other people's kids during preschool meltdowns, a first-ever wasp-sting, a particularly grave bike crash, and that howling windstorm up on Chena Dome.

There is no right answer here, other than, "Proceed with caution, results may vary."

Coöpting Other People's Kids

All the kids—aged eight to eleven—had lighters, matches, and knives.

There were at least three campfires going on the little gravel bar, and children were running back and forth with tinder, dry sticks, larger downed wood, and actual logs. Saws waved about. Willow sticks were being sharpened to accommodate a wide range of roastable or maybe-roastable foods. In other words, it was par for the course for our annual Spring Family Campout. And, I noticed, none of the little people seemed to be tired—no matter how far they biked.

Granted, most of this pack of friends had arrived by car. This was, after all, an unapologetically car-camping-type weekend, here at the Upper Chatanika Campground. What started years back as a whim has grown into a tradition: in mid-May, sometime around my birthday and Mothers' Day, when the ice is just barely out, the gravel bar just barely snow-free, and the mosquitoes not yet a force to be contended with, we go to hang out with a bunch

Biking to the Spring Family Campout

Location ▪ Upper Chatanika Campground, Steese Highway, north of Fairbanks.

Distance and duration ▪ 95 miles round trip, one overnight.

Locomotion ▪ Biking, with one kid on a tag-along behind an adult, one kid on a tandem bike with an adult, and an older kid on her own bike. Gear in panniers, additional gear brought by those driving to the event.

Terrain ▪ Variable, with one very large hill.

Weather ▪ Sunny and pleasant spring conditions, about 50-60°F.

Accommodations ▪ Tent camping at campground. Treated water from river, firewood gathered for open campfires. Outhouses.

TIP ▪ Self-Entertaining

The older kids get, the less you have to worry about keeping them entertained, because they will have found ways to do that themselves. This is especially true if the group includes not only siblings, but also friends. Three or more tweens or teens may not even want you intruding on their conversations and hilarity.

If trail games are needed, simple ones like Twenty Questions can become deviously complex Infinite Questions, in which the answer might be, for example, the Statue of Liberty's left pinky finger. Our gang has enjoyed Categories, in which players take turns, from A to Z, trying to think of an item that fits a theme agreed upon by the group, such as "fruit" or "clothing" or "things from Harry Potter." You will not win this game.

For quiet, dull, tired, in-the-tent times, entertainment remains crucial. But now you can select it based on your own interests as well as theirs. Are there card games everyone likes? Word games? Silly games? Many board games can be trimmed of their boards for lighter travel (e.g., Pictionary), and books for reading aloud or reading independently are always important. Charades, Yahtzee, Set, MadLibs, and anything that can be played with a standard deck of cards all offer great possibilities.

of delightful adults, children, dogs, whatever. We make no attempt to be efficient or light-weight in our packing, and we are perfectly content with only-semi-wilderness joys at a state-managed campground. There are outhouses and places to park and unsuspecting other Fairbanksans who didn't anticipate QUITE so many kids this early in the season.

But because our traditions are never quite normal, there are also always bikes leaning against trees. Our bikes—but also, because insanity is oddly catching, other bikes, too. Over the years, we've been joined on this ride by many of the usual suspects, including Tom and Amy, and a few less common candidates like Margaret and David. This particular year, we enjoyed the company of a friend's kid—aged eleven-and-eleven-twelfths. Not under duress, I swear.

The Upper Chatanika Campground is about fifty miles from our house. The ride there is beautiful and lightly trafficked. It includes lots of level ground and lightly rolling hills—and one tremendous whopper of a hill: Pedro Dome. Switchback after switchback, liberally decorated with signs warning trucks of 6%, 7%, and 8% grades, the road over Pedro climbs inexorably for more than five miles.

The year in question, Molly and Lizzy were eight-almost-nine. Molly and I were on our then-brand-new tandem, her feet just barely reaching the rear pedals. Lizzy, shorter legged, was on a tag-along behind Jay. Ezra, aged eleven, proudly rode his shiny new full-size adult bike.

The agreement was for the rest of the family, coming by car, to ferry Ezra home the next day. But still, this was biting off a lot. Coöpting others into adventures they would not otherwise have imagined is both delightful and worrisome—doubly so when those people are kids. Are you SURE you want to bike fifty miles, kiddo? Once you say yes to that question, it can be hard to change your mind. Torturing children is really not on my agenda as a fun activity. So, although I've frequently stuck my neck out to take along extra kids on steep grueling hikes, chilly lengthy ski trips, or arduous sweaty bike rides, I still hesitate every time.

But in this case, I shouldn't have worried. Young Ezra was—and is—a highly determined individual. At not quite twelve, this child was unwilling to show weakness, tiredness, or regrets. I could tell, at some points that it was a hard push. Really hard. But there was no grousing about it.

Our ride was already paced, to some degree, to meet the needs of kids. Our own two, of course, had the advantage of not having to entirely pull their own weight. That meant that Jay and I were not moving at the speed we would have done on our own, which made us a better match for a strong Big Kid. Plus, although the bulk of our camping gear was being transported by friends—including Ezra's parents, Laura and Paul—we had pannier bags with extra clothing and snacks for everyone, while the lone child rider was unencumbered. And we took more breaks than we would have done on our own. One of those breaks, at the convenience store in the small outpost of Fox, involved buying everyone ice cream bars. It always does. Tradition is important.

Now, watching all the kids run around the gravel bar with pyromaniacal joy, it would have been hard to tell which three had spent hours in the saddle. No one appeared to have low energy, tired legs, or a sore butt. Everyone was working on creating the perfectly browned marshmallow. End of story.

Except that, in this case, it wasn't.

The following morning, as the campout was starting to wind down after another session of pyromania, and a long breakfast that morphed into brunch, I expected the not-yet-twelve-year-old to gratefully load the bike onto the carrier strapped to the back of the family car. Instead, I was informed that that, contrary to the original plan, our borrowed kid wanted to bike back, with us.

And so it was. Giant hill, ice cream stop and all.

But How Do You Deal with . . .
Getting Big Kids to Dress for the Cold

"What's the temperature?"

"Oh, pretty warm today! Seven above."

Seven above. Yes, we talk this way.

On a trip to New York some years ago, Molly and Lizzy were amused by the general ongoing panic about the weather. It was, locals contended, ungodly cold. The kids countered that this was clearly not the case, given that the temperature was, in all cases, a positive integer. Indeed, they were predisposed to be mocking: "You think this is cold? This isn't cold!"

Aside from noting the impropriety (and potential risk) associated with mocking New Yorkers, I also pointed out that if one is not dressed for the prevailing conditions—if, indeed, one does not own the necessary apparel— then it can indeed feel ungodly cold at plus seven Fahrenheit.

Plus seven. See, there it is again.

Fahrenheit positivity is not assumed, because for long stretches of time, it's rare. For the months of December, January, and February, average temperatures in Fairbanks are below zero. During a cold snap the temperature can drop below negative forty—which, incidentally, is the crossover point at which the Celsius and Fahrenheit scales coincide. Every other temperature requires an F/C conversion, but minus forty is just . . . minus forty.

So we say "plus seven." Fairbanks children learn about negative numbers long before they learn about multiplication and fractions. Dealing with temperatures this mind-bogglingly frigid requires it. It also requires mental preparation, logistical know-how, and several pairs of long johns.

It's important to be properly dressed for an afternoon stroll on the local trails near our home. FAMILY PHOTO

In an attempt to evoke empathy, I explained to my kids that in New York, people don't own long underwear. Like, not even one pair. Not even the lame cotton kind. Children might not even own snowpants, and adults almost certainly don't. Neck warmers? Thick wool socks? Triple-layer mittens? Sorels, Lobbens, or mukluks? Afraid not.

Well, okay, the twins agreed, that would be a problem. They were sympathetic up to a point, but they were too cynical to accept this not-owning-stuff premise as the only problem. "What about that time when none of Sylvia's friends had coats?"

They were recalling a different visit, when we hit Boston during a cold snap. The mercury was hovering around zero, and the wind was singing a not-so-merry tune. Meeting the twins' cousin and her friends at middle school, we set off to walk home with a posse of kids.

My two, despite not having brought their "real" winter clothes, and despite being puny little seven-year-olds at the time, were doing fine in mid-weight jackets, hats, mittens, and rain pants over their ordinary outfits. In contrast, the pre-teens were suffering. Some suffered in silence, and others were drama-queen shrieking, but no one was happy.

This wasn't because they didn't own jackets and hats. These were not sadly abused or neglected kids. Twelve-year-olds in Cambridge Massachusetts own such things. They were suffering because they hadn't brought their warm clothes to school. Apparently, warm clothes were not cool. Dude.

I'll attest that this pack of kids looked decidedly less cool wearing bits and pieces of my borrowed apparel and shivering their way into a coffee shop where I (suddenly aunt to half a dozen) fortified everyone with hot chocolate and croissants. Those numb red fingers and ears? Definitely not cool.

It's easy to laugh at the fashion lunacy of middle-schoolers, but I've observed adults who don't do much better. Granted, most of them have figured out that they should probably don at least some winter wear. They pull on their puffy jackets or stylish long woolen coats, and then can't fathom why they are still cold. This problem would be solved by pulling up their hoods. Oh. Wait. Their jackets don't have hoods. Why don't their jackets have HOODS?

Even among adults, it seems that hoods and hats are uncool. They mess up hairstyles. They are unfashionable. I'd like to smugly label peer pressure as a "kid thing"—but nope. All too often, when we think we're dressing for the cold we aren't REALLY dressing for the cold. Instead, we are putting on what society—or some sub-section of society—has told us to wear when it's cold out. Some-times, this means we're wearing too many warm layers. Sometimes, it means we're wearing too few. Often, it means we're wearing the wrong ones.

Those shivering middle-schoolers may be rebelling against memories of being forced to wear hot, bulky snowsuits (think A Christmas Story), when energetically tumbling around in compar-atively balmy 30°F snow as small children. My childhood memories of snowball flights and sledding suggest these events were surpris-ingly sweaty.

In most cases, poor clothing choices are uncomfortable, but not tragic. Inadequately clad seventh-graders can take refuge in coffee shops. Sweaty little snowman-builders can simply come inside and create snowy puddles and piles of damp laundry. But inadequately clad cross-country skiers can find dead white patches on cheeks or toes, and sweaty backwoods adventurers can find their cooling sweat freezing to the insides of their jackets as the sun goes down.

In short, owning the right gear is important. Knowing when to put it on, and when to take it off, and when to put it back on again is an art form. And not caring what the other middle-schoolers think—that's a Jedi mind trick.

Marathon Girls

"Mom, we'll be fine!"

So the twins had told me that morning. At that point, the skies had been leaking a cold and relentless drizzle as the crowds had gathered at the Equinox Marathon starting line at the university soccer field. But now, I was at the top of Ester Dome, the twins and their friend were some unknown distance behind me on the trail, and it was snowing and sleeting sideways. As I jogged and speed-hiked my way up and down the steeply undulating ridgeline trail known as the "out and back," I pulled my sleeves over my hands—and wondered if the kids had been smarter than me, and still had their mittens.

Equinox Marathon

Location ▪ Greater Fairbanks area, including Ester Dome.

Distance and duration ▪ 26.2 miles; 10-hour time limit.

Locomotion ▪ Jogging and hiking with mini packs for emergency gear and snacks.

Terrain ▪ Very hilly, with over 3,000 feet of elevation gained and lost; trail well marked.

Weather ▪ Cold light rain, turning to snow at higher elevation.

Accommodations ▪ Organized race; aid stations with water and energy drinks about every two miles.

The Equinox Marathon is such a quirky Fairbanks event that an entire book has been written about its history, from 1963 to the present. It's a marathon, yes—a 26.2 mile footrace. But its focus from the outset was not so much on elite athletes and record-breaking speed, but on creating a challenging local event for Fairbanksans. Its originators were particularly focused on encouraging high school-aged participants. In early years, it drew dozens of boys and girls in roughly equal numbers—during a time when most marathons didn't permit female entrants at all.

> I had been feeling bad about all the junk food we were eating on the marathon until I turned around and saw the woman behind us squirting honey right into her mouth from an 8oz bottle. I didn't ask if she planned to drink the whole bottle during the race.
> *–Lizzy, amused by the quirks of adults*

Over the years, the event drew in more adults, and more serious runners, but it remained an open-hearted community celebration of the great outdoors. I participate year after year, not because I'm fast, but because I feel so welcome not to be. Slow joggers are welcome. Hikers are welcome. Amblers are welcome. Indeed, everyone is welcome—including small gangs of free-ranging children with plenty of snacks and plenty of determination.

The twins, aged thirteen, were out on the trail with their twelve-year-old friend, Laurel. Their entirely self-defined goal was to hike the course in under ten hours—the cutoff for being an "official" finisher.

I was ahead of them—by how much I had no idea—moving faster than a hiking pace, but not setting any ground-speed records. This was September 21st. The wind was buffeting the mountaintop. The trail was damp and slightly slick. It was snowing on me. It was also, presumably, snowing on the kids.

They'd be fine.

They had far more warm clothing with them than I did. They'd prepared for this event, via an enthusiastic self-imposed regimen of long family day-hikes. Jay was planning to check on them by bike at two different road crossings. Laurel's dad, David, would catch up with them at a later juncture. If anything went wrong in between, there were plenty of folks out on the course, including other racers and stalwart cheering fans. Indeed, I was impressed to see the usual number of supporters, despite the weather.

On or near the autumnal equinox each year, the Equinox Marathon winds along trails and dirt roads, luring its participants through 3285 feet of elevation gain and loss. Usually, it offers gorgeous views of the golden birch leaves that crown our too-brief fall season. Sometimes, it offers a foretaste of winter.

> Laurel commented that the inside of her right knee was hurting, she could not straighten her leg all the way. Of course, the only thing that made it feel better was to keep running.
> —Molly, on persevering

Between mile fifteen and mile sixteen, I reached the turnaround point for the out-and-back, and a larger water station that also offered snacks. It was being hosted by a herd of middle schoolers, Laurel's classmates, and overseen by her mom, By. As I paused to grab a couple of cookies, the two of us exchanged a few words.

How were the kids doing, we wondered? They'd be fine, we concluded.

The last ten miles of the race include a lot of downhill. This sounds good, until you try it with tired legs and aging joints. Lots of people tend to pass me on the downhill. In other years, Jay has brought the twins to a spot between mile twenty and mile twenty-one, to hand out mini doughnuts and gummy candy, and to cheer on the slogging runners. This year, of course, they weren't there. No worries, though. Other people, of their own free will and on their own dime, were passing out snacks along the course—and in a couple of locations, beer. I've never sampled the latter, but I'm fully in favor of taking candy from strangers—and encouraging my kids to do the same.

I staggered across the finish line five hours and twenty-three minutes after the starting gun went off. The fact that this put me sixth out of the twenty-four female participants aged 45 to 49 demonstrates that this is not an elite event. Normally, my first thought would have been a sandwich, and my second would have been a shower. This year, I had other things on my mind. Luckily, Jay was there to fill me in. The kids, he said, had already made it past the snowy mountain—miles ahead of meeting their ten-hour goal. They were doing a lot of jogging interspersed with their hiking, and were warm, fed, hydrated, and in good spirits.

By the time I'd had my sandwich and my shower, it was time to get back to the finish line—which, after 26.2 hilly, challenging miles, is in the same place as the start.

And there they were, descending the final slope and coming across the damp green soccer field. They looked small. They looked muddy. They looked determined, tired, and happy. They sprinted in, of course.

The girls had completed their first marathon in seven hours and thirty-four minutes. When I congratulated them and told them how impressed I was, they rolled their eyes. Had I really thought they couldn't do it? They were insulted. And perhaps rightfully so. After all, they'd told me they'd be fine.

Acknowledgements

The advice and stories in this book represent a group project, co-created over many years by all the friends who have shared adventures, misadventures, and everyday outdoor fun with us— including those who are mentioned in these pages, and those who are not. We appreciate your energy, your initiative, your ideas, your trust, your knowhow, and your good humor.

Much appreciation is also due to those who read drafts of this manuscript, in part or in whole, including Amy Marsh, Phyllis Morrow, Robin Barker, Sandra Boatwright, Lou Brown, Diana Saverin, and Dana Greci. Special thanks to everyone at UA Press, particularly Krista West and Nate Bauer for their tireless encouragement, copy editing, and expert advice; to Tom Moran, who provided photos and detailed feedback, and to Otto Kitsinger, who offered editorial assistance on many of the essays herein, as well as professional advice regarding photography.

Finally, we'd like to thank our own parents, Charlotte and Jay Cable Sr. and Janet and Robert Fresco, for teaching their own kids, many years ago, about the joys of playing outside.

About the Author

Nancy Fresco lives in a cabin on the outskirts of Fairbanks, Alaska with her husband, Jay, and their twin daughters, Elizabeth and Molly. Whenever possible, they disappear into the wilds to enjoy the many forms of playing outside described in this book, including bike touring, hiking, cross-country skiing, snow-biking, and pack-rafting. Their hobbies also include caring for a collection of rescue pets, attempting to garden, undertaking assorted building projects, curling up with a good book, and, of course, writing.